A Postage Stamp History of Canada

A Postage Stamp History of Canada

Victor Seary

McGraw-Hill Ryerson Limited

Toronto
Montreal New York London Sydney
Johannesburg Mexico Panama Düsseldorf Singapore
Rio de Janeiro Kuala Lumpur New Delhi

ISBN 0-07-077327-0

1 2 3 4 5 6 7 8 9 10   AP-72   10 9 8 7 6 5 4 3 2

Library of Congress Catalog Card Number
74-39022

Printed and bound in Canada

The author and publishers acknowledge with
thanks the kind assistance of the Empire Stamp
Company, Toronto, for supplying stamps used
in illustrating this book.

Introduction

The world's first adhesive postage stamp was issued in Great Britain on May 6, 1840. It was printed in black ink, carried a picture of Queen Victoria and cost one penny. There were no perforations to allow the stamps to be separated easily one from another. They had to be cut apart with scissors or a sharp knife.

Postal services had existed for centuries. The Chinese had an efficient courier service as far back as the Chou Dynasty (1122-255 B.C.) and Roman couriers carried despatches back and forth over the famous post roads of the Empire. The system in use in Europe and North America before 1840 provided for the carriage of letters from place to place by mail coaches and the person receiving a letter paid the costs of its carriage and delivery. These charges were high and varied according to the distance the letter had been carried and, rather oddly, according to the number of sheets of paper in the letter. Some people could not afford to get many letters because the delivery charges were too expensive.

In England this problem of high postal charges caught the interest of a clever and inventive man named Rowland Hill. As a young man he had been a schoolmaster — at the age of twelve he was teaching mathematics in a school run by his father, who had developed a new and improved system of education. One feature of this system was "to leave as much as possible all power in the hands of the boys themselves." It proved to be a very successful system and Hill ranks with the great Arnold of Rugby as an educational reformer and educationalist.

He was obliged by bad health to give up teaching and brought his active mind to bear upon other things, among them the invention of an improved printing press, schemes for colonizing Australia, and public questions, including the reform of the postal service. Hill argued that if the price of delivering letters were sharply reduced many more people would use the postal system, so that the government would not lose revenue. He showed that the cost of delivery varied so little with the distance a letter was carried that a single uniform charge for delivery anywhere in the country was both possible and fair, and he suggested that the charge should be one penny. He also proposed that the sender of a letter, not the receiver, should pay the cost of delivering it. He even explained how this might be done "by using a bit of paper just large enough to bear the stamp, and covered at the back with a glutinous wash which by applying a little moisture might be attached to the back of the letter."

These ideas were strange and startling to people at the time, and the government of the day did not receive them with any enthusiasm. It took two years of argument and persuasion before the government accepted Hill's suggestions and adopted "penny postage," and it did so only because public opinion had been aroused to support Hill and others who agreed with him.

So delighted were people with the introduction of penny postage that poems, none of which, it must be admitted, added much lustre to English literature, were written about it.

> *Hail joyous day! The Postage Bill*
> *Brings blessings, great and many,*
> *And best of all say what we will,*
> *It only costs a penny.*
> *From John o' Groats to England's end*
> *From Norfolk to Kilkenny,*
> *A letter now may reach a friend,*
> *And only cost a penny.*

From that time until he retired, in 1864, Sir Rowland Hill was, except for a short interval, a civil servant employed in the Treasury and in the Post Office. He had the satisfaction of seeing the volume of mail in Britain increase from seventy-six million letters in 1838 to six hundred and forty-two million in 1864. When he retired Parliament gave him £20,000. He died in 1879 and was buried in Westminster Abbey, the tomb of many of Britain's greatest sons.

No one knows when stamp collecting as a hobby began but it was probably quite soon after the invention of postage stamps. So many of the original British penny black of 1840 were preserved that it is still possible to get a good used copy from a dealer for less than $25.00. As other countries began to issue stamps only gradually it was possible for a few years for a collector to acquire a specimen of every stamp in the world. But more and more countries adopted the idea of cheap postage, and the numbers of stamps issued by each country also greatly increased so that the hope of building a complete collection of the world's postage stamps became an impossible dream.

Nearly every man in the English-speaking world has collected stamps at some time in his life, some estimates putting the figures at ninety out of a hundred. Girls are perhaps less likely to be attracted by philately but about one woman in twenty is, or has been at some time, a collector. The overwhelming majority of these people, becoming collectors in childhood, collect anything and everything. There is a flood of stamps available — colourful, bizarre, of all shapes and sizes. They come from scores of countries, some of them so small and distant that they are practically unknown, but every government of an independent state knows and appreciates the use of postage stamps as a medium for promoting trade and commerce, attracting tourists, advertising natural resources, recording its history or advancing its political and cultural ideas. Some countries make additional revenue by issuing more highly coloured and attractively designed stamps than their postal requirements actually demand. These stamps are really issued for sale to collectors and the practice is shoddy and unethical.

The general collection has many attractions, the great-

The 1951 reproduction of the three-penny beaver of 1851.

est being, perhaps, its endless variety. For those who are dismayed by the quantity of stamps available, and by the hopeless dream of ever completing a collection of them, there remains specialization. Sooner or later the more serious collectors select some one country, some one type of stamp, or some topic of interest, and concentrate on it. Here, too, it may be rarely possible to gather all the examples one might wish but the specialized or topical collection provides satisfactions the general collection cannot offer. So there are collections made of stamps showing birds, fish, insects, animals or flowers, buildings, ships, sculpture or paintings, heraldic designs, games and athletics, famous men, and on and on. The list of possibilities is limited only by the imagination and ingenuity of the collector himself.

This book endeavours to show how one country, Canada, has created through its postal issues its own history in pictures. Granted this history is incomplete. There are gaps in it. Some areas, notably literature and the arts, have so far been rather neglected. Many notable Canadians and many Canadian events still await their turn for commemoration on stamps, but the bold outline of our history is there.

The first postage stamps issued by British North American colonies appeared in 1851 — Canada, Nova Scotia and New Brunswick all issuing stamps that year. These three colonies were to unite, in 1867, to form the first of the great British "dominions," self-governing countries that changed over the years from colonies to independent nations. The stamps they issued in 1851 are now rare and valuable to varying degrees. The twelve-penny black stamp carrying a portrait of Queen Victoria, issued by Canada, might cost the collector, if he could find one for sale, perhaps $10,000 or more.

The first stamp illustrative of Canadian history is not

The three-penny beavers of 1851 and 1858, and the five-cent beaver of 1954.

one of the queen's portraits or the beautiful floral emblem and crown designs from Nova Scotia or New Brunswick, handsome and rare though they are. It is the Canadian red three-penny stamp of 1851 showing a beaver. The beaver has for a long time been a symbol in the heraldry of Canada, and this is appropriate because it was the industrious beaver that really made Canada important to Europeans and induced them to come and establish settlements, or at least trading posts. Beaver pelts were at first taken back to France to be used simply as furs, but it was soon discovered that the soft, short inner fur of a beaver pelt, once the long, coarse, outer guard hairs had been removed, could be made into a superb felt. Gentlemen in Europe wore felt hats and the very best felt hats were those made of Canadian beaver. The demand for beaver pelts became so great that they joined spices, sugar and tobacco as one of the imports most eagerly sought by European merchants and manufacturers.

The history of the seventeenth century in Canada and what are now the Northeastern States of the United States, is mostly the history of the fur trade. The rivalry of French and English to gain control of the sources of supply and to persuade the Indians to trade exclusively with one side or the other led to bitterness and war. It also led to the establishment of great trading companies such as the English Hudson's Bay Company established in 1670 and the French *Compagnie des Indes* which was given a monopoly of the fur trade in New France in 1717.

An interesting fact about Canada's first stamp is that it was designed by Sir Sandford Fleming (1827-1915). This remarkable man had come to Canada from his native Scotland only six years before, and during his long lifetime was to build much of Canada's great railway network, devise the system of time zones, work toward the linking of the various countries of the British Commonwealth by a state-owned system of telegraphs and in many other ways leave the mark of his energy and imagination on the country. So far he has not been honoured by having a postage stamp issued in commemoration of his services to Canada.

The stamp he designed is now rare and expensive and so is another beaver stamp, the five-cent red issued on July 1, 1859, when Canada gave up the old currency of pounds, shillings and pence and adopted the dollar and decimal currency. Fortunately, a picture of the three-penny beaver of 1851 appears on the fifteen-cent bright red, or scarlet, stamp issued in 1951, centenary of postage stamps in Canada.

Exploration

We shall probably never have a single clear account of the discovery and first exploration of what is now Canada. Early records have been lost or perhaps were never written at all. There are legends that cannot be proved to be based on truth and stories from one country that conflict with those from another. There is a Portuguese legend, for example, that America was really discovered by a fisherman, Afonso Sanches of Cascais, a little port not far from Lisbon. His ship was blown far off its course, so far indeed that it reached the land across the Atlantic. Sanches and two or three of his men managed, more dead than alive, to struggle back to Madeira where they were cared for by a certain Genoese navigator named Columbus who was living there and to whom they gave an account of their experience, as well as their ship's log with all the information it contained.

There is no longer any doubt that Norse adventurers sailed their long ships down the coasts of Newfoundland, and perhaps those of Nova Scotia and New England, about five hundred years before Columbus sailed on his epic voyage to the West Indies. The details of their travels and of the landings and settlements they made seem to be forever lost and all we have is a vague outline.

The first voyage of discovery to our shores about which we have some fairly reliable information is that made in 1497 by an Italian navigator, John Cabot (Giovanni Caboto), under the authority of close-fisted Henry VII of England. Henry granted John Cabot and his three sons, Lewis, Sebastian and Santius, "full and free authority, leave and power upon their own proper costs and charges, to seek out, discover and find whatsoever isles, countries, regions or provinces of the heathen and infidels, which before this time have been unknown to all Christians." A further provision gave the king 20 per cent of any profit made on the voyage, which was shrewd of the king since he had been careful to arrange for the Cabots to bear all the expenses.

An 1897 Newfoundland set: the ten-cent Matthew, *the two-cent* Cabot, *the sixty-cent* Henry VII.

Cabot sailed from Bristol some time in May, 1497, in the little ship *Matthew* with a crew of seamen from that port who, it seems likely, had already been across the Atlantic in search of new fishing grounds. He reached land and went ashore on June 24, St. John the Baptist's Day, and took possession of it in the name of Henry VII. All English claims to ownership of this part of North America are based on this act of Cabot. Having established England's claim to "the New Found Land," Cabot sailed for a month, a voyage of three hundred leagues from west to east and, driven by a west wind, sailed from the cape of the mainland nearest Ireland to Brittany in fifteen days and thence to Bristol.

It is difficult to decide just where it was that Cabot landed. Before 1956 it was generally thought to be the northern point of Cape Breton Island or, as recent authorities insist, some point on the coast of Newfoundland. Cabot, of course, thought it was the northeastern coast of Asia. A letter written in 1497 or 1498 by the English merchant John Day to a correspondent in Spain, whom he addresses as "Almirante Mayor" and who was quite possibly Columbus himself, gives a detailed account of Cabot's voyage. This letter, which was found in 1956, when studied together with maps made shortly after the voyage, indicates that the actual landfall may have been farther west, somewhere on the south shore of Nova Scotia or even, perhaps, on the coast of Maine.

Wherever it was it made Cabot a famous man. He gladdened the hearts of the Bristol men with his tales of the sea swarming with cod, for in those days before refrigeration salt cod was a most important winter food and the demand for it was never-ending. The king, never a careless man with money, gave him £50. In fairness it must be said that in those days a skilled workman — a carpenter or shipwright — would work a sixteen-hour day for little more than a penny, and a ship

The Newfoundland five-cent Cabot in the Matthew *(1947), and the Canada four-cent* Matthew *(1949).*

of about two hundred tons capable of carrying a crew of captain, boatswain, cook and sixteen seamen could be bought, exclusive of rigging and fittings, for about £30. It was not a lavish gift but it was not as meagre as appears at first glance.

One of Cabot's fellow countrymen who was living in England wrote home to say that Cabot "is called the Great Admiral . . . and goes dressed in silk and these English run after him like mad." It was well he had his brief moment of glory because his next voyage seems to have turned out badly. No record of the voyage remains but references to it indicate that he never returned, and one writer callously remarked that "he is believed to have found the New Lands nowhere but on the very bottom of the ocean, to which he is thought to have descended together with his boat. Since that voyage he was never seen again anywhere."

Men spoke of the land Cabot had visited as the "New Found Land." When Newfoundland joined Canada in 1949 to become the tenth province, Canada marked the occasion by issuing a four-cent stamp carrying a picture of Cabot's ship the *Matthew*. Fifty-two years earlier Newfoundland issued a set of stamps with the double purpose of celebrating the four-hundredth anniversary of its discovery and the diamond jubilee of Queen Victoria. In the set the two-cent bright rose stamp bears the portrait of John Cabot, "Him that found the New Isle," the ten-cent sepia or dark brown a picture of the *Matthew* and the sixty-cent black a portrait of Henry VII. There is considerable doubt whether the picture of the *Matthew* on the stamp is accurate. The printers used a picture of the same ship as that on a three-cent stamp issued in 1893 by the United States, where it is described as "the flagship of Columbus"!

The ten-penny Cartier of 1855, the seventeen-cent Cartier of 1859, and the one-cent Cartier and Champlain of 1908.

Although John Cabot vanished in 1498, the word of his discoveries quickly reached other European countries, and encouraged them to send out expeditions of their own. Gaspar Corte-Real, a Portuguese, and his brother Miguel were in North American waters by 1500/01. Giovanni da Verrazzano, a Florentine in the service of France, cruised the coasts of Nova Scotia and Cape Breton in 1524 and at least went ashore long enough to kidnap an unlucky Indian lad to take back to Europe. Cabot's story that the codfish were so plentiful they could be dipped out of the ocean with a basket brought the Basque, Portuguese and French fishermen as well as the English to the Banks of Newfoundland. They may, indeed, have been coming there even before Cabot died.

Jacques Cartier was born at St. Malo in Brittany in 1491 but nothing is known of his early life. He was apparently an experienced navigator, for in 1534 he was given command of two ships, carrying sixty-one men, and sent off by France to find a northwest passage to the East.

He crossed the Atlantic in twenty days, from St. Malo to the coast of Newfoundland. This was a fast voyage for the times and the kind of ship employed. Passing through the Strait of Belle Isle Cartier made a circuit of the Gulf of St. Lawrence, searching for a passage to the west which would take him to China, and always was disappointed. The north shore of the Gulf was so unattractive to him that he said it must be "the land God gave to Cain," but later he reached Prince Edward Island and remarked that it was "the best tempered region one can possibly see, and the heat is considerable." He did not discover that it was an island. He mistook the Magdalen Islands for part of the mainland, and he did not pass Anticosti Island and therefore failed to find that the St. Lawrence was a river and not just another bay.

He did encounter some Iroquois and took two of them

The 1934 three-cent Cartier and the twenty-cent Cartier Arrival at Quebec, issued in 1908.

back to France so that they should learn French and become translators on later voyages. When he returned the next year they came with him. This time he sailed with part of his men up the St. Lawrence to an island where there was an Indian village called *Hochelaga* which was a fortified town of the Iroquois. Near it was a mountain Cartier named *Mont-Royal*. Autumn was well-advanced when he left this, the future site of Montreal, to return to the Indian town of *Stadacona* (Quebec) where his men were building a fort and preparing to spend the winter. It was a terrible winter and Cartier's ships were locked in the ice for five months as the St. Lawrence froze all the way to Hochelaga. Scurvy and privation caused the death of a quarter of the French and more would have died if Cartier had not persuaded the Indians, who were now tired of the French and becoming hostile, to tell him how cedar sprigs steeped in boiling water could be used as a remedy.

Early in May 1536 Cartier returned to France taking with him the chief Donnacona and nine other Iroquois, not all of them willing guests. His second voyage had been a very successful and satisfactory one in spite of the bad winter experience. He had discovered the vast river with all the promise it held for future discoveries, even of a route to Asia. The Indians had told him of huge fresh water seas and kingdoms where copper and other valuable minerals were plentiful and he actually had a few gold samples and good furs to show what the new country produced.

Because France was at war with the Emperor Charles V, it was five years before Cartier made his third and last voyage. The Indians he had taken home in 1536 had all died and he had no interpreters. Welcoming at first, the Indians soon became suspicious and sullen. There is some indication that they besieged the French camp all winter and killed a number of Cartier's men, but the records of this expedition are incomplete and no one now knows what really happened. He left in June for France carrying with him what he believed to be gold samples and diamonds, but they proved to be iron pyrites, or fool's gold, and quartz crystals — a cargo of dreams that did not come true.

Cartier lived until 1577 but he went on no more voyages of discovery and the French government, troubled by civil wars and perhaps disappointed by his "gold" and "diamonds," sent no more important expeditions to Canada for another sixty years.

Canada has issued five Cartier stamps. Three of these carry his portrait as imagined by artists and the other two are scenes of his arrival at Quebec. Two of these stamps are over a hundred years old. They are the ten-penny blue of 1855 and the seventeen-cent blue of 1859. They are obtainable but are far from common. In 1908 Canada issued a set of stamps to celebrate the three-hundredth anniversary of the founding of Quebec. The one-cent blue-green of this set carries the familiar Cartier portrait along with that of Samuel de Champlain, and the twenty-cent yellow-brown is a picture of Cartier's ships before Quebec in 1535. In 1934 a three-cent blue stamp was issued, on July 1, to commemorate Cartier's first voyage ending on Canadian soil. France also issued two stamps celebrating the voyage of 1534.

. . . . .

While the French seemed to lose interest in American exploration in the sixteenth century, the English remained eager for further discoveries and the wealth that might be gained from them. It was the Age of Elizabeth, a time when Englishmen showed great energy and ambition in so many undertakings. They looked on the sea as a highway that led to fortune, fame and the possessions of the Spanish enemy, which lay ready for the taking by anyone bold enough to dare.

One such seaman was the Yorkshireman Sir Martin Frobisher. The date of his birth is not known exactly, but according to one account he first went to sea at the age of nine. On a later voyage to Guinea he was held prisoner by an African chief for some months. One who knew him described him as being "of great spirit and bould courage and naturall hardnes of body." By the time he was about thirty he was referred to as Captain Frobisher and for the next few years was a typical swashbuckling daredevil such as the Elizabethan Age produced in great numbers. He was a privateer who sometimes omitted to get a licence and was three times accused of piracy, though never brought to trial.

There was much talk during Elizabeth's reign of possible routes to Cathay either by a northeast passage or a northwest one. Frobisher's interest was caught and for fifteen years he tried to persuade wealthy people to provide him with ships and supplies so that he could go find the Northwest Passage and open a trade route with the Far East.

Finally he succeeded, getting the support of the Muscovy Company which gave him a licence to explore a northwest passage, while one of its directors helped him to get the necessary ships. He set sail with the *Gabriel*, of about twenty tons, and the *Michael*, of perhaps twenty-five, together with a pinnace — a cockleshell carrying four men — which was lost with all hands in a great storm off Greenland. The remaining two vessels were separated by the storm, and the *Michael* returned home while Frobisher in the *Gabriel* pushed on to the west.

Frobisher gave it as his opinion that "the Sea at length must needes have an endyng, and that some lande should have a beginning that way." On July 28, 1576, he sighted the coast and shortly afterward discovered "a greate gutte, bay or passage," which he thought was a strait dividing Asia on the north from America on the south. He named it "Frobisher's

The ten-cent Newfoundland Annexation (1583-1933), and the Canada five-cent Frobisher and the Gabriel issued in 1963.

Strait" but it was actually the large bay in Baffin Island now called Frobisher Bay.

He took home some mineral samples which one assayer claimed, either through ignorance or for some reason of his own, contained gold. This created so much interest that two other expeditions went out under Frobisher's command, one in 1587 and another in 1588. The third expedition was driven by a storm into what Frobisher, annoyed by the mishap, described as "mistaken straytes." He sailed into this "strayte" for nearly two hundred miles before turning back and therefore failed to find Hudson Bay as he might have done.

As it became clear that the ore he had carried home contained no gold, Frobisher lost interest. There were so many things to do. He sailed with Drake on a privateering raid to the West Indies that made him a rich man. He fought against the Armada and was knighted for his services. He joined Drake again and harried the Spaniards wherever he could find them and he died in 1594 of wounds got while fighting them in France.

The five-cent ultramarine stamp carrying his portrait and a picture of his little ship, the *Gabriel* was issued on August 21, 1963.

. . . . .

Another Elizabethan eager to find the Northwest Passage to Cathay was a man different in every way from Frobisher. This was Sir Humphrey Gilbert, a son of well-to-do Devonshire gentry. Where Frobisher went to sea as a small boy and grew up a tough and daring sea-dog, Gilbert went to Eton and Oxford and became a courtier. He entered Parliament too, and wrote a book on the existence of the Northwest Passage and how to find it. He had ideas on trade with the

The Newfoundland one-cent portrait of Sir Humphrey Gilbert and the fifteen-cent Gilbert on the deck of the Squirrel, *both issued in 1933.*

natives and the founding of colonies in America; but his theories were a mixture of wisdom and foolishness because he lacked any real knowledge of North American geography.

Gilbert was a man of sudden enthusiasms. He joined a scheme for the production of copper by the transformation of iron into the more valuable metal. He led an English army to the Netherlands to help the Dutch in their rebellion against Spain, but accomplished little; so he came home and busied himself with various other plans for colonizing Ireland, creating a new kind of university and posing as an authority on America.

Spurred on by the accounts of Frobisher's first voyage, he got permission from Queen Elizabeth to organize a great expedition to sail to America, fight the Spanish in the West Indies and find and colonize some suitable part of the North American coast.

In November 1578 he had gathered a powerful squadron at Plymouth and set sail for America. In order to fill out his crews he had got a number of men out of prison, among them men awaiting trial, or actually condemned, as pirates. There was always something absurd or comic about Gilbert's projects and this one was like the others. His expedition had no sooner set sail than three, and eventually four, of his ships sailed away to resume their profession as pirates. The remainder of the squadron, some of the ships leaking, put in to Cork Harbour. Later they struggled out across the Atlantic, turning back one by one as new disasters struck them, until only the *Falcon*, commanded by Gilbert's younger half-brother Walter Raleigh, remained. Finally even Raleigh gave up and sailed back to Plymouth. The whole expedition was a gigantic failure and Gilbert had succeeded only in losing his fortune and that of his family.

Gilbert, however, refused to give up. Five years later

he had put together another expedition, this one with the aim of colonizing the North American coast at *Norumbega* (near Narragansett Bay, Rhode Island). He planned to stop on the way and take formal possession of Newfoundland for Queen Elizabeth. He set out with five ships from Plymouth on June 11, 1583, and after a slow voyage during which his best ship, the *Bark Raleigh*, commanded by Walter Raleigh, got into difficulties and turned back, the other four vessels met outside the harbour of St. John's on August 3. There were thirty-six fishing craft at St. John's — English, French, Basque and Portuguese — and they were inclined to resist Gilbert and keep him out of the harbour because they recognized one of his ships as a former privateer which had attacked some of them the previous year.

Gilbert, arrogant and full of confidence as always, flourished his commission from the Queen, and the English fishermen gave way and let him enter. He then assigned shore stations to fishermen, issued licences to permit them to continue fishing in the neighbouring seas and took their provisions in order to replace his own which had been used on the voyage.

Next he took formal possession of Newfoundland and the lands within two hundred leagues north and south of it and proclaimed it to be the Queen's forever. He also proclaimed some remarkable laws of which he was the author. Anyone who showed disrespect for the Queen, for example would lose his ship and goods and have his ears cut off as well.

Having arranged things at St. John's to his own satisfaction — we are not told what the fishermen thought — he set sail once more for Narragansett. On the way he overruled his experienced captains as to the course to take, with the result that the ships got in shallow water off Sable Island and one ran ashore and broke up, drowning part of her crew. This event so discouraged the crews of the remaining vessels that it was decided to return to England without delay.

Gilbert himself was sailing in the *Squirrel*, a little frigate of only ten tons. Autumn was coming on and the Atlantic was stormy. His captains advised Sir Humphrey, who had hurt his foot, to leave the *Squirrel* and come on one of the larger ships, but Gilbert refused their advice and returned to the dangerously overloaded little *Squirrel*. They ran into very heavy weather, strong winds and the short, high seas of an angry Atlantic. During a lull those on one of the larger ships got close enough to the *Squirrel* to see and hear Sir Humphrey. He was seated on deck with a book in his hand and he called out to them repeatedly, "We are as near to Heaven by sea as by land." Later that night watchers on the other ship saw the lights of the *Squirrel* suddenly go out. Gilbert was gone, and it might be said of him as it was later of King Charles: "Nothing in his life became him like the leaving it."

. . . . .

Sir Humphrey Gilbert had had plans to establish a settlement, or perhaps several settlements, in America. Until his time explorers usually looked on the lands they found after crossing the Atlantic as a barrier shutting them off from their real goal, which was the fabled East with all its riches. So they sought a passage through or around the land mass that stood between Europe and the East. Gradually a new set of ideas arose. Perhaps there was no Northwest Passage, but America itself might be made to produce wealth. It might provide a home for Europeans as well. So while Cabot, Cartier, Corte-Real, Frobisher and the others came and went, taking home the ores and minerals they hoped would bring quick wealth and which always disappointed them, the new men beginning with Gilbert began to seek out suitable places for Europeans to live.

Perhaps the greatest of these new men was Samuel de Champlain, who was an administrator and colonizer as well as an explorer. And exploration has never ceased in Canada

The 1958 five-cent Champlain and view of Quebec, and the 1908 fifteen-cent Departure for the West.

since the day Cabot first sighted the coast. Down through the years the explorers have sought different things, first the Northwest Passage, then sources of the best furs, gold and silver, oil and radium, right down to the times in which we live.

Champlain first came to North America in 1603 with Gravé du Pont, a naval officer turned merchant who had first come to Canada in 1600 as a trader at Tadoussac. He explored the lower reaches of the Saguenay and heard from the Indians of a great salt water sea (Hudson Bay) far to the north. He also went up the St. Lawrence for a considerable distance but found nothing that was not already known through the journeys of other Frenchmen who had preceded him.

In 1604 he was back, this time as geographer and unofficial second-in-command to the Huguenot Pierre du Gua, Sieur de Monts, who hoped to find in Acadia a more suitable climate in which to establish trading operations and build a colony. He explored the Bay of Fundy and the adjoining coasts including the Penobscot area, in what is now the state of Maine, and the mouth of the Saint John River.

He also chose winter quarters for the expedition. This was Ile Sainte-Croix (now called Dochet Island) in the St. Croix River. In the warm and sunny autumn days it seemed an ideal place, but the winter that followed was a bitter one and thirty-five of the party died before Spring, largely from scurvy. It is remarkable that each group of newcomers seemed to be ignorant of what had happened to earlier exploring parties. Sir Winston Churchill said that those who failed to learn history were obliged to live it over again. If Champlain had been familiar with the accounts of Cartier's experiences seventy years earlier he would have known how to cure, or at least to combat, scurvy.

The one-dollar Champlain monument, Quebec (1935), and the five-cent L'habitation de Québec (1908).

In the Spring of 1605, after searching the coast as far south as Cape Cod, De Monts moved the colony to Port-Royal (Annapolis Royal, N.S.) and Champlain made careful maps of the entire journey. The next two winters he spent in comfort bordering on luxury at Port-Royal while in the summers he engaged in a leisurely examination of the coast of New England, and in 1607 the coast of Nova Scotia, so that the whole Atlantic coastline from Cape Breton to Cape Cod was charted.

De Monts had now lost his monopoly of trade in Acadia, and Champlain, as his lieutenant, returned to the St. Lawrence where in 1608 he chose "the point of Quebec" as the site for a habitation or settlement — several buildings surrounded by a palisade of logs and a moat.

Here, too, winter proved to be disastrous. Twenty-five Frenchmen formed the population in the autumn and by spring sixteen of them, including the doctor, were dead of scurvy. Even before winter closed its iron grasp on the little settlement there had been serious trouble. Jean Duval, a locksmith who had been at Port-Royal with Champlain and who had been a disorderly trouble-maker on at least one earlier occasion, had a dream of sudden riches. He persuaded several other discontented members of the party that they could kill Champlain and sell the new habitation to the Spanish, or the Basques. The plotters were betrayed by one of their number who grew frightened and decided to try to save his own skin. So Duval was hanged and his head stuck up on the highest and most visible part of the fort to serve as a warning to others.

Treason and scurvy made Quebec's beginning a discouraging one. But Champlain persisted with his plans and in the summer of 1609 set out to find the country of the Iroquois. He went up the Richelieu River and, with only two other

Frenchmen and a few Indians of the Huron, Algonkin and Montagnais tribes, pushed on southwards past the Chambly Rapids to the beautiful lake that now carries his name.

It was here that he made a serious error in judgement that was to have tragic results for the French and help to cost them possession of Canada. He and his men attacked the Iroquois. It was an unequal battle because the French had firearms and the Iroquois had not. Although they were beaten and ran away, leaving their dead chiefs behind them, the Iroquois never forgot nor forgave and in all the years that were to come of struggle between French and English the Iroquois remained the most steadfast of France's enemies.

For the next few years Champlain acted as the lieutenant in Canada of a succession of French aristocrats who remained at home, leaving him to run the affairs of the colony. He returned to France in the autumns to report to these grandees, but spent part of each year exploring the interior of the country and working to extend and increase the fur trade with the Indians.

One of these journeys (1612) took him up the Ottawa River and across-country for some distance. Three years later he again went up the Ottawa but this time he also ascended the Mattawa to Lake Nipissing and thence down the French River to Lake Huron. He was delighted both with the enormous lake and with the fertile country of the Huron Indians, but more was to come. On he went, south to Lake Simcoe and east by slow stages, making friends with the Indians as he went, to the eastern end of Lake Ontario. Crossing Lake Ontario, Champlain and his Hurons pushed south into what is New York State until they reached an Iroquois fort, or palisaded village, not very far from the present city of Syracuse. The Hurons rushed to the attack but were driven off, while Champlain was wounded in the knee by an Iroquois arrow and had to be carried on the long retreat back to Lake Simcoe where he expected to pass the winter. Recovering from his wound, he travelled during the winter studying the Indian customs and way of life in the country east of Lake Huron.

Although he had now seen more of America than any of the earlier explorers and visitors, Champlain still believed that Asia might be just over the next hill. In 1618 he wrote to the King of France that one could easily reach "the Kingdom of China and the East Indies, whence great riches could be drawn," by way of New France and that customs duties on these rich goods could be collected at Quebec. But his own days as an explorer were pretty well ended. The remainder of his time in Canada was filled with the problems of settlement, the rivalries of fur traders, the politics of the French court and the task of governing the vast territory now called New France. It was a life filled with worry and he must often have despaired that the colony he had founded would ever amount to anything. In 1629 he had been obliged to surrender Quebec to Sir David Kirke, the Anglo-French leader of an expedition that set out to displace the French in Canada. When England and France patched up peace again in 1632 he had to rebuild Quebec. In the midst of all this work, and while still planning great things for the colony and war with the Iroquois, he became ill, suffered a stroke and died on Christmas Day 1635. His portrait appears on the one-cent green stamp issued as part of the Quebec Tercentenary set, and on the five-cent green and brown stamp of 1958, but it is based on guesswork. No authentic portrait of Champlain exists; in spite of the many books he wrote and the full accounts we have of his actions and of his plans for the country he had come to love so completely we do not really know what he looked like or much about him as a person.

. . . . .

The country between the Ottawa River and Lake Huron, all

The five-cent Dollard des Ormeaux, issued in 1960.

that area visited by Champlain in 1615, became the source of the furs upon which the prosperity of New France depended. The Indian tribes there, mainly Hurons and Algonkins, traded with the French, and French missionary priests were successful in converting many Indians to Christianity.

The colony was gradually acquiring settlers, many of them engaged in the fur industry in one way or another. Three Rivers, or Trois-Rivières, was set up as a trading post in 1634; Montreal was founded in 1642 and began to grow, even though its location near to the country of the Iroquois discouraged the more recently arrived newcomers from France.

Nor were they mistaken if they were wary of the Iroquois. This powerful group of allied tribes had been supplied with firearms by the Dutch who had settled New York and gradually set up trading centres and settlements up the Hudson River and along its tributary, the Mohawk. Having cleaned out most of the beaver and other fur-bearing animals in their own country, the Iroquois began to trap north of Lake Ontario in what was the territory of Indians friendly to the French. Small bands of warriors often accompanied the trappers and interfered with cargoes of furs being carried by Hurons to Montreal or some other French post. In modern times we should call these raids "highjacking."

This struggle to control the fur trade kept alive and strengthened the hostility that had begun with Champlain's attacks on the Iroquois thirty years earlier. A kind of war, undeclared but deadly, was being fought all the time.

It was in this state of affairs in 1660 that a young soldier-settler in Montreal, Adam Dollard des Ormeaux, hit upon a plan to strike a blow at the Iroquois raiders that would dishearten them and check their activities and, at the same time, permit the passage down the Ottawa to Montreal of large cargoes of furs trapped during the previous winter by the

The ten-cent Indians stretching skins, issued in 1950.

Indians of the Ottawa and Mattawa valleys. He gathered a little party of daring young men — the oldest was thirty-one, the youngest ten years younger — to accompany him up the Ottawa where they might hope to ambush an Iroquois band of trappers or warriors. What he did not know, although there had been rumours of a major attack by Indians on the French settlements, was that several very large war parties had already arrived. There were perhaps as many as five hundred Mohawks and Oneidas at the mouth of the Richelieu River and a big war party of Onondagas up the Ottawa.

It was this strong Onondaga band of two or three hundred warriors that Dollard met at Long Sault on May 1, 1660. The Hurons who accompanied the seventeen Frenchmen knew at once that this was not a small party of Iroquois raiders but a powerful war party and advised Dollard to retreat at once to Montreal. But the French had found an old Algonkin fort and decided to make a stand behind its palisades.

They were given no time to strengthen the flimsy defences of the fort because the Iroquois attacked at once, interrupting Dollard and his men as they were eating a meal. After some exchange of musket fire the Onondagas proposed a truce which the French accepted. Unfortunately, while the parley was taking place, someone in the fort broke the truce by shooting at the Iroquois. Infuriated by what they believed to be treachery, the Indians renewed their attack. They also sent to the Richelieu for reinforcements from their allies gathered there. The siege continued for seven or eight days — accounts differ — but there would be only one ending. The Hurons nearly all deserted at the first opportunity. Dollard's men were all either killed or wounded, except five whom the Onondagas captured in a final rush. One was tortured to death on the spot and the other four were taken back to meet a similar fate in the villages of the Mohawks, Oneidas and Onondagas.

One other result of the battle at Long Sault was that the Iroquois gave up their plans for an immediate mass attack on the French settlements. This was probably not because of their lost warriors, for these only amounted to a score or so out of a force of six or seven hundred or more. They were always easily turned aside by some omen or accident and on this occasion they had four prisoners to display, a good many scalps, and a victory to boast about.

Dollard and the fight at Long Sault were forgotten as time went on — it was only one more of the many heroic and bloody encounters between French and Indian. Then, about the middle of the last century, an old manuscript history of Montreal was discovered and the tale of "The Seventeen" was taken from it and retold in terms that made Long Sault comparable to Thermopylae. It was not. But it was a heroic episode in our history in which we may take pride. Dollard des Ormeaux appears on a five-cent ultramarine and brown stamp issued in 1960, three centuries after he made the military blunder of being caught in a trap by a superior force and redeemed it by the courage with which he paid for the mistake. In addition, he accomplished what he set out to do, for the Iroquois went home, and a short time later Pierre Radisson, the famous *coureur de bois*, whom the English knew as "Mr. Radishes," ran a load of furs worth 200,000 livres into Montreal.

. . . . .

Not very long after the Hudson's Bay Company began operations in the Bay, in 1670, there arrived at Port Nelson trading post an English boy named Henry Kelsey. He was fourteen when he reached Port Nelson and he was acquainted with Pierre Radisson and with Jean Baptiste Chouart, the son of

The six-cent Henry Kelsey, issued in 1970.

Radisson's partner Groseilliers.

The management of the Company believed the Indians would come down the rivers emptying into Hudson Bay and bring their furs to trade at the Company's forts. Some of them did, but the French urged them to by-pass the English and send their peltry to Montreal. It soon occurred to the Hudson's Bay Company people that someone should be sent inland to persuade the Indian trappers to continue to come to Company posts, and perhaps to find as well additional tribes with furs to barter.

The man hit upon to undertake this project was young Henry Kelsey. He was now about twenty and in the years since his arrival he had become a skilled hunter, one who could travel wilderness trails enduring the hardships such a life imposed better than the Indian youths who were his companions.

During the next two years, 1690-1692, he made his way inland through the lakes and rivers between Hudson Bay and Lake Winnipegosis. He was the first European ever to see the Canadian prairie and probably the first ever to see and hunt buffalo. He went some distance up the Saskatchewan and set up a trading post, but his story is vague, at least partly because he chose to record his wanderings in very bad verse, a kind of doggerel that reminds the reader of West Indian Calypsos:

This wood is poplo ridges with small ponds of water
There is beavour here in abundance but no Otter.

The forced rhymes, the frequent use of inappropriate or incorrect words, blurred his images and obscured his records so that we are not able to determine just where he did go. His reports, even later ones in prose, vanished into the archives of the Company and it was not until 1926 that his papers came to light again.

In 1970, the three-hundredth anniversary of his birth, a six-cent multicoloured stamp was issued showing his head outlined by the prairie sky, and carrying the inscription in both English and French, "First explorer on the plains."

. . . . .

The Hudson's Bay Company had been operating on the west shore of the Bay since getting a charter from Charles II in 1670. The Company carried on a valuable trade with the northern Indian tribes but its operations were always in danger of interruption every time France and England were at war. This happened often enough for the Company to try to safeguard its trading posts by making them capable of defence. In 1731 it decided to make Churchill its main stronghold and sent a gang of masons and skilled tradesmen there to build a stone fort, Fort Prince of Wales.

It was from this place that the H.B.C.'s servant Samuel Hearne (1745-1792) set out in 1769 to find the river in the North West from which the Indians from time to time brought pieces of raw copper, as well as copper implements and ornaments, to trade with the Company. Rumours of its existence had stirred the interest of white fur-traders for fifty years. Hearne was also to search for a Northwest Passage, or a River of the West, leading to the Pacific, the old exciting dream that had beckoned men on for two hundred years or more. As the Company's employee he was, of course, also expected to persuade the Indians to take their furs to Churchill.

Hearne's first two attempts to carry out these tasks were failures. He was a gentle, rather timid, man quite unable to exert his authority over the Indians who accompanied him. They ignored his orders and stole his possessions, even taking his gun. His first trip ended in about a month, while the second, though it took nine months, resulted in little but a gain in experience. The Indians took him on a great figure-of-eight journey through the barrens northwest of Churchill. He learned to travel light, to live off the land even on the tundra where game was scarce and wary, and where, since there was often no firewood and the tundra mosses were dripping wet, it was often necessary to eat raw flesh, usually fish or porcupine, or go hungry.

He had one great success. He met and made friends with a remarkable Chipewyan, the capable, clever and loyal Matonabbee. This man believed that the Company's efforts to preserve peace among the Indian tribes, even though it was a policy of self-interest, was worth his support and he urged the Indians to do their trading at the H.B.C. post at Fort Prince of Wales.

When Hearne started out for the third try to find the copper mines and the northwest passage out of Hudson Bay, Matonabbee went with him. His presence guaranteed Hearne's safety and success. He took several of his wives with him, five or six strapping women each of whom, he boasted, could do the work of several men. Hearne agreed with this estimate of their ability, but was rather shocked at the rough treatment they got. Matonabbee took care of all the details of the journey, the hunting of game, the construction and carrying of light canoes, the setting up of camps and all the other matters that Hearne, left to himself, would have bungled. The party grew as it went along. Matonabbee's relatives and friends, a considerable clan, joined it and so from time to time did other Indians of different tribes. Some were ready to help Hearne find copper, but the real purpose of most of them was to launch an attack on their traditional enemies, the Eskimos. They did find and surprise one Eskimo hunting-party and massacred the members while the ineffectual Hearne looked on in horror.

The six-cent Samuel Hearne with a map of the Coppermine River, issued in 1971.

Shortly after this episode Hearne was led to some rocky little hills where a few fragments of native copper were found. One piece weighed four hundred pounds and was eventually sent to the London office of the Company. But there was neither enough of the metal nor any satisfactory way of transporting it so that the economic value of the discovery was little. The mouth of the Coppermine River where it empties into Coronation Gulf was located on his return journey. Hearne followed the river's east bank south, thence west of Lake MacKay and across the eastern arm of Great Slave Lake. A little south of Great Slave he turned east and went straight across-country to Churchill. He proved there was no northwest passage out of Hudson Bay since if there had been he must have crossed it either on his outward journey or on his return. He thought one of the useful results was to show that the continent was much wider than many people had thought. In all his wanderings during nearly nineteen months he did not meet an Indian who had ever visited the west coast or had ever seen the western sea.

Hearne became governor of Fort Prince of Wales a few years later and was taken prisoner by the French when they captured it in 1782. The fall of the Hudson's Bay Company stronghold and the capture of his friend threw Matonabbee into such despair that he hanged himself.

In 1971 Hearne's exploit was celebrated by the issue of a light tan stamp bearing his name and dates in red. It shows a map of the Coppermine River and the date of its discovery, 1771.

· · · · ·

A few years after the battle at Long Sault there arrived in Montreal from France a young man named René-Robert Cavelier. He had spent nine years in the Jesuit order, but his superiors had not found him a satisfactory member, while he confirmed their opinion by resenting and opposing the Society's rules, by his lack of discretion, his bad judgment and instability. When he asked to be released from his vows they were happy to oblige him.

He was as unsatisfactory a settler as he had been a Jesuit. Dreaming of glory and hoping to discover a way to the Southern Sea and thence, of course, to China, he sold the land given him on Montreal Island and set out to find the Ohio River. He went with two companions whom he had untruthfully told he could speak the language of the Iroquois. He was also supposed to know enough astronomy to do the navigation required, but he knew scarcely more astronomy than Iroquois. He was not the only ill-equipped member of the party, however. The man who was to be the cartographer knew very little about maps. Nor did any of these three "leaders" have the slightest idea of how to survive in the woods. Setting out with a flotilla of nine canoes at the beginning of July 1669, they reached a spot near the present city of Hamilton by the end of September.

Here they broke up and Cavelier set out, he said, for Montreal. But he did not go there and no one really knows what he did for the next year or two. It was said he had discovered both the Ohio and the Mississippi but this is almost certainly not so and there has never been any evidence that he did.

He was deeply in debt and friendless when in 1672 the Comte de Frontenac arrived in Canada as governor general. Cavelier supported the new governor in his difficulties with his subordinates and with the Jesuits. The two hot-tempered, arrogant, quarrelsome men somehow got on well together and Frontenac became Cavelier's patron. Through the influence of the governor he obtained possession of Fort Cataraqui (Kingston, Ontario) which he renamed Fort Frontenac. He also secured rank as a noble with the title *de La Salle.*

Able now to push on with his schemes for exploration, La Salle built a small vessel above Niagara Falls and named it the *Griffon* after a heraldic beast that formed part of Frontenac's coat of arms. Within six weeks of its launching the *Griffon* vanished, probably sunk in a sudden storm on Lake Michigan, leaving La Salle more deeply in debt than ever.

During the years that were left to him La Salle explored and set up forts in Illinois, bustling backwards and forwards to Montreal, making treaties with Indian tribes, arguing with his creditors, finding jobs for a growing number of relatives and complaining that his enemies were plotting against him. His first great achievement was in 1682 when, with a few French companions and some Indians, he sailed down the Mississippi past the point where the river's discoverers, Marquette and Jolliet, had ended their voyage, and onwards to the river's mouth. In April 1682 he took possession of Louisiana in the name of the King of France.

During the next five years he struggled to establish a new, strong French colony in Louisiana and to plan for an attack on the Spanish in Mexico. Frontenac was gone and his creditors in Canada were pressing him. It was to France and the King that La Salle now turned for assistance in the carrying out of his schemes, and Louis XIV eventually fitted out an expedition for him, complete with soldiers and a thirty-six-gun warship. They sailed for the mouth of the Mississippi, but because La Salle was still as unskilful an astronomer and navigator as he had been on his first exploration, they could not find it. Months of searching failed to reveal it and the continued disappointment brought many of his followers to consider mutiny. The warship sailed back to France leaving La Salle to fend for himself. His long-felt fear that people were plotting against him this time proved true. The plotters killed his nephew, and, when La Salle hurried to the spot to investigate, shot him from ambush. His feverish and disorganized

The five-cent Cavelier de La Salle, 300th Anniversary, 1966.

pursuit of fame and fortune ended in the tangled undergrowth and mud of the Mississippi Delta.

On April 13, 1966 Canada issued a five-cent bluish green stamp marking the three hundredth anniversary of La Salle's arrival in Canada.

. . . . .

On June 4, 1958, Canada issued a five-cent bright ultramarine stamp in honour of Pierre Gaultier de Varennes, sieur de La Vérendrye, the great explorer of much of Canada west of the Great Lakes.

Gaultier, or La Vérendrye as he is best known, was born at Trois-Rivières, P.Q., in 1685. The Gaultiers were a French family of quality and René Gaultier, the father of Pierre, had come to Canada in 1665 with the famous Carignan-Salières Regiment and, like many officers and men of that unit, had chosen to remain in Canada on lands granted them by France when the regiment went home. He died in 1689 leaving eight children for whom places had to be found. The eldest son went at once into the French army and Pierre, when he was old enough, at twelve years of age, became a naval cadet. The War of the Spanish Succession, "Queen Anne's War," broke out in 1702 and the usual barbarous Indian raids on border settlements began again. La Vérendrye, at the age of nineteen, as a cadet in the French marines took part in the bloody attack and massacre at Deerfield, Massachusetts, and a few years later sailed to France and joined the Regiment of Brittany as a junior officer. He was just in time to take part in the battle of Malplaquet (September 11, 1709), the last of Marlborough's great victories over the armies of Louis XIV. La Vérendrye was wounded and taken prisoner and as the war was ending he returned to Canada, his military career ended.

He turned to fur-trading to make a living and in 1727, when he was middle-aged, he was made assistant commandant of the Northern Posts, three French trading-post forts built at strategic points across the North where they could cut off the Indian trappers with their cargoes of furs and prevent them from going to the Hudson's Bay Company's factories.

One of these Northern Posts was at Kaministikwia (Thunder Bay, Ontario), and it was here that he met Indians who told him of great rivers and lakes further west and of the routes by which they could be reached. For a long time the French had been interested in a mysterious Sea of the West, and the Indians told La Vérendrye that it could be reached by means of the lakes and rivers they described to him. Vérendrye proposed the establishment of a trading-post on the shore of Lake Winnipeg with the idea of using it as a base for explorations searching for the Sea of the West.

In Paris, the Minister of Marine and Colonies, the Comte de Maurepas, gave his approval provided La Vérendrye's schemes did not cost very much. So for the next twelve years La Vérendrye and his four sons searched and traded across the West. Three months or more of travelling separated them from Montreal. They had canoemen to pay and maintain. The Indians had to be won over by generous gifts. And in France Maurepas grew impatient for word of the Sea of the West but offered little or no funds.

The La Vérendryes struggled on as best they could, paying expenses by trading in furs but going steadily into debt. Lake of the Woods, Rainy Lake, the Red River, Lake Winnipeg and Lake Manitoba became familiar to them. They went up the Assiniboine, and explored the Saskatchewan past the fork and up to about where the present city of Saskatoon sits on its banks. They went down the Missouri and finally crossed the Bad Lands, circling the Black Hills and coming within sight on the western horizon of the Big Horn Mountains — the outposts of the Rockies.

The five-cent La Vérendrye, issued in 1958.

They met and traded with Indian nations never known before, Shoshones, Gros Ventres, Cheyennes, Crows, Assiniboines, the deadly Sioux who were bitterly hostile, and those strange "white" Indians, the Mandans. La Vérendrye's oldest son, with a number of followers, was killed by a Sioux war party. His nephew died on the trail. None of this counted with M. de Maurepas. He wanted his Sea of the West, if it existed, and since La Vérendrye could not find it someone else had better do so. La Vérendrye was recalled to New France and spent the last six years of his life nearly penniless. He died on December 5, 1749.

He had said, "I am only seeking to carry the name and arms of His Majesty into a vast stretch of countries hitherto unknown, to enlarge the colony and increase the commerce." In 1938 a monument was erected at St. Boniface, Manitoba, in honour of La Vérendrye. Its Latin inscription, translated, reads "He found these lands and opened them to humanity and to faith." A bronze heroic figure of the explorer stands looking toward the west. Beside him stands a missionary priest holding high the Cross and before them crouches an Indian shading his eyes against the light of the sunset. The Canadian stamp issued in 1958 has taken this monument as a model for its design.

The Treaty of Paris in 1763 put an end to French rule in Canada and at the same time it ended French control of the fur trade and French exploration of the great empty country across which the La Vérendryes had made their adventurous way. Many of the wealthier French and those of standing in New France abandoned the country after the surrender of Montreal and returned to France. It is a tragic footnote to history that many members of the La Vérendrye family including Pierre, La Vérendrye's youngest son, were drowned when the *Auguste*, the ship in which they were sailing to France, was lost in 1761 in an Atlantic storm.

It was only a short time however before the British, using Montreal as a base, took up both fur trade and exploration — the two went hand in hand — where the French had left off. To Montreal came shrewd New Englanders, sharp traders and hard bargainers by tradition and training. There they were joined by Scotsmen and Englishmen like the Yorkshire-born brothers Joseph and Thomas Frobisher, all men who had an urge to collect wealth and who were prepared to take risks and face danger in order to acquire it.

These were the people who were prepared to defy the Hudson's Bay Company and compete with it for the furs in the great Northwest and the markets in Europe. Half a dozen Montreal companies soon had men working west of Lake Winnipeg. It was only a short time before these separate companies united to form the North West Company. From its foundation in 1779 until it united with the Hudson's Bay Company in 1821 the North West Company gave the older company the sternest possible competition, and in the struggle of these greedy giants to control the fur trade of half a continent there emerged a band of explorers and adventurers who revealed Western Canada to the world.

There was Peter Pond, the morose, illiterate American who was probably a murderer but who found the way to the Athabaska, and Alexander Henry, another American, who broke into the Churchill country. There was the great Sir Alexander Mackenzie, first to reach the Pacific by land from Canada, and Simon Fraser who explored from the Peace country of northern British Columbia to the mouth of the river that carries his name.

· · · · ·

In many ways Mackenzie was the greatest of the explorers who filled in the map of Canada. He had great courage and determination that drove him to persist in his plans and over-

The six-cent Alex Mackenzie, issued in 1970.

came every obstacle in his way. He won and held the respect of his men and though he was a hard driver he never expected others to work harder, take more risks or endure greater fatigue than he did himself. He was, in fact, a superb leader.

He was born in the little town of Stornoway in the Hebrides, probably in 1764, though there is some doubt about the date. When he was about ten, his mother having died, he was brought to New York by his father, who had a brother living there. At the outbreak of the American Revolution his father, who had been a junior officer in the army opposed to the Jacobites in 1745, and his uncle, both joined a Loyalist unit, The King's Royal Regiment of New York. Young Alexander was sent to Montreal to be out of harm's way and probably never saw his father again, for the elder Mackenzie did not survive the war.

In Montreal, when he was old enough, Alexander entered the employ of a small fur-trading firm. By the time he was twenty he was sufficiently trained in the details of the fur trade to be sent by his employers first west to Detroit and then to the Churchill country to trade with the Indians. In 1785 he was made a partner in the business. Two years later he and his friends joined the North West Company and Mackenzie was awarded one share in the new enterprise — representing 10 per cent of the ownership.

He was chosen, and it is evidence of how highly the partners in the North West Company regarded him, to go to Fort Athabaska to take over command of the trading post from the formidable Peter Pond.

Pond was twice his age, a bitter, bad-tempered and dangerous old soldier who had been at Ticonderoga in 1758 and who had marched as an officer in Amherst's army to Montreal and the final defeat of the French in Canada before Mackenzie was born. Pond and Mackenzie spent the long winter of 1787/8 shut up together in Fort Athabaska. If Spring did not find them close friends neither did it find them enemies. Pond had given Mackenzie a great store of knowledge, legend and theory about the country. His information had been gained by personal observation, the reports of his men and by a careful piecing together of accounts given him by the Indians. He had also drawn maps which proved to be wildly inaccurate, particularly about distances, but which gave a kind of general view of the country west to the Pacific.

When Spring came Pond set out for Montreal, which he shortly left to return to his old home in Connecticut where he was to die in undeserved poverty and obscurity in 1807. He was the man who turned Mackenzie's thoughts to the search for a way to the Pacific.

Mackenzie's first move was to abandon Pond's old headquarters on the Athabaska River and establish himself at a new post, Fort Chipewyan on the north shore of Lake Athabaska. His cousin Roderick was placed in charge of the fort and the ninety or more employees, while Mackenzie gave his full attention to his plans for an expedition to the Pacific. The discovery of a route to the Pacific might make it possible to ship furs home to Britain by sea and free the traders in the Northwest from the long tiresome journey back to Montreal. This, with Mackenzie, was perhaps a secondary reason, even a rationalization, for the real reason, which was the passion for discovery, the fame to be won by being the first to reach the Pacific by an overland route.

Whatever it was that drove him — ambition, hope of additional profits, new trapping areas to exploit or a mixture of all three — he set out on the morning of June 3, 1789. It was a small group of nine men and four women. Two of the Canadian voyageurs had brought their wives, while English Chief, the Indian who was to combine the duties of interpreter and hunter, brought two wives.

They left the western end of Lake Athabaska —
thence down the Slave River to Great Slave Lake. On the way
they had trouble with ice, driftwood and bad weather and
lost one of their canoes in a rapid. The lake itself was covered
with ice except near the shore and they were unable to make
any progress for many days. Food was no problem. There
was an abundance of fish, and they killed geese, ducks and
swans whenever they wished. The women gathered berries
and occasionally brought in a clutch of duck or goose eggs
as well. One of their more severe hardships was the attacks
of ferocious insects which Mackenzie called "Muskettows and
Gnatts," the latter being the Canadian springtime scourge, the
black fly.

It was June 29 before they managed to reach the river
flowing out of the lake, the river they hoped would take them
to the Pacific. Swept along by the powerful current they sometimes covered a hundred miles or more in a day. At first the
river flowed west-by-north and the mountain range became
clearer, a great barrier, its peaks lost in the clouds, shutting
them off from the west. Gradually the river's flow changed
from the earlier promising direction to one that veered steadily
toward the north.

Once they found some Indians living on the river's
bank and Mackenzie, with English Chief as interpreter, tried
to get information from them about what lay ahead. He got a
story about impassable falls and strange monsters, and the
estimate that it would take several years to reach the sea. This
left Mackenzie unperturbed, but frightened English Chief so
badly he wanted to take his wives and go home. Mackenzie
had trouble persuading him to continue. Indians joined them
from time to time to act as guides. The rapid pace was maintained so that towards the middle of July they were in
Eskimo country in the delta of the river. They found debris
of Eskimo encampments, broken sleds, bones and other dis-
carded material, but saw no Eskimo. By July 13 they had

reached tidal water and seen white whales, and on the next day Mackenzie set up a record post on the island where they were encamped. He named the island "Whale Island" and carved his name, the number of men with him and the date on the marker post. It was July 14, 1789, and on that day the Paris mob attacked the Bastille and launched the French Revolution which was to involve the Western World in war for the next twenty-five years or more.

Supplies were short and the pemmican they brought with them was mouldy. There were no Eskimos available for information and Mackenzie was aware of the short duration of the Arctic summer. It was time to go. The long paddle back against the current of the river took them until September 12, when they reached Fort Chipewyan.

His discovery of the course of the river that now bears his name and his pursuit of it to the Arctic aroused little or no interest among his partners in the North West Company. His territory of Athabaska sent in a rich harvest of furs and that was all they asked. But Mackenzie himself was less easily satisfied. He had set out to find a way to the Pacific and he never turned back from anything he wanted to accomplish.

So in 1792 he was back from a visit to England with new navigating instruments and with his plans made for another journey on another river. Pond's map showed the Peace River flowing into Great Slave Lake. Actually it joined the Slave River not far from Lake Athabaska, and Mackenzie's plan was to go up the Peace in the autumn of 1792 to an advanced base, spend the winter there and set out early in the spring of 1793 for the trip into the unknown lands beyond.

By May he was ready to start. Six canoes loaded with furs obtained from the Indians during the winter were sent back to Fort Chipewyan. A splendid new canoe had been built to carry his party westwards. It was light enough for two men to carry, yet big and strong enough to carry a ton and a half of goods and provisions together with ten people. The ten were Mackenzie, an assistant, Alexander Mackay, six Canadian voyageurs and two Indians. The course the expedition was to follow would take them up the Peace until it came to a point where two tributaries joined it. One, now called the Finlay, came down from the northwest. The other, the Parsnip, flowed up from the southeast. Fairly trustworthy information from an Indian indicated the southern tributary as the one to follow. Once its headwaters were reached it should be possible to carry over the height of land and put the canoe in a stream flowing westwards to the sea.

To follow this plan proved to require effort almost beyond the strength and endurance of the party. Continuous falls and rapids, the river squeezed between the towering walls of canyons, made the journey as dangerous as it was exhausting and discouraging. The canoe was constantly requiring repairs. Portages miles long had to be made along paths hacked out of tangled forest, deadfalls and burnt-over areas. Some days the forward progress amounted only to a mile or two, and for three weeks the average was not much over ten miles a day, every inch gained by back-breaking work.

They finally won their way across the height of land, the great continental divide separating the waters that flowed east from those running toward the Pacific. Mackenzie and Mackay were thus the first Europeans to cross it north of Mexico. A short portage brought them to a river flowing roughly in the right direction but it was filled with rapids that wrecked their already sadly battered canoe which had now been so patched and smeared with gum and resin that it was heavy and hard to manage. It was a tributary of the Fraser and they were soon in that great river itself.

They now began to encounter Indians, people very different from those east of the mountains. Some of them were guardedly friendly. Others were actively hostile, sending flights of arrows whistling past them. Mackenzie's own Indians helped him get information about what lay ahead from some of the friendlier local tribesmen. It was not very heartening and Mackenzie decided to go back up the Fraser to a point where an Indian trail led almost directly west and, leaving a new canoe they had built and some provisions, strike for the coast on foot.

This march took fifteen days during which they were passed from one Indian band to another. The enormous trees, the unfamiliar customs of the Indians with their diet of salmon and their elaborately carved and painted totems and longhouse decorations fascinated Mackenzie and his voyageurs. The nearer they got to the coast the more insolent the Indians became and it was necessary to take care not to stir them to violence. Mackenzie and his men reached a village of friendly Indians on the Bella Coola river about thirty miles from the sea. These people lent them canoes and a guide the next day, and two days later they saw the sea. The coast Indians were very threatening but Mackenzie stayed long enough to get day and night observations so that he could calculate the latitude and longitude. This was accomplished on a rocky headland in Dean Channel. His observations completed, he made a kind of paint by mixing vermilion with melted grease, and with this he printed on the rock in large letters the brief notice reproduced on the brown six-cent stamp issued in 1970:

Alex Mackenzie/from Canada/by land/22d July 1793

He was only thirty. He had added a vast area to the map of Canada and he and Mackay were the first Europeans to have crossed Canada to the West Coast. Now, as an explorer, his work was done, the Northwest Passage had been found at last and it was a passage by land. The rest of his career was one of increasing fame but his travels were over. He was knighted in 1802. He served in the legislature of Lower Canada and he opposed Lord Selkirk's plan to settle the Red River country. In 1805 he returned to Britain to stay,

The five-cent David Thompson, with map of western Canada, issued in 1957.

and for many years he tried to persuade the British government to set up posts and establish control of the Pacific coast at least as far south as the Columbia River. Even the prestige given him by the success of his books on his explorations and his undoubted great knowledge of North American conditions failed to stir the British. That Paris mob that rioted on the day he reached the Arctic Ocean had begun a revolution and the revolution had had an heir — Napoleon. Britain's struggle with Napoleon was a life-and-death affair and there was neither time nor energy left for the establishment of trading companies on the other side of the world, profitable and strategically advantageous though they might be. His achievements were complete in themselves, and yet the final step, for which they provided the path, was never taken. Mackenzie died early in 1820 convinced that the hardships he had experienced had fatally ruined his health and, in one respect at least, he died a disappointed man.

· · · · ·

And finally there was David Thompson, a Welsh orphan boy who left the Grey Coat School in Westminster to enter the employ of the Hudson's Bay Company, where he was to remain for fourteen years. During his years with the Hudson's Bay Thompson became an excellent surveyor and a close observer of plant and animal life. As a trader for the Company he quickly learned all about the Indians. Before he was thirty, Thompson had travelled over nine thousand miles of inland waterways and had accurately surveyed a third of them. But his salary was small, his superiors gave him no encouragement and there seemed little prospect for promotion. So he left the Hudson's Bay Company and joined the rival North West Company.

Britain had just signed the Jay Treaty (1794) defining the border between British North America and the United States. Thompson's first duty as a Nor'Wester was to check on where this new boundary ran and make sure the North West Company's trading posts were on the right side of the line. During the next year he travelled four thousand miles, on foot, on horseback, by canoe and on snowshoes, completely circling Lake Superior as well as visiting the Mandan country.

The next year he visited the Athabaska country, married a half-breed girl and traded successfully with the Indians. The Company was anxious to find a way to the Pacific and Thompson was the man it believed most likely to find one. So year by year he continued searching. In 1803 he was at Lesser Slave Lake. By 1807 he had crossed the Columbia River and explored its upper valley. He traced the Kootenay to its mouth in Kootenay Lake, and he discovered Athabaska Pass before, in 1811, reaching Astoria, the American post at the mouth of the Columbia. Then he surveyed the whole course of the Columbia.

Easily the best geographer and map maker of the time in America, his last professional task was to survey the United States-British North American border from Lake Superior to Lake of the Woods as a member of an international commission set up for the purpose. During his career as an explorer he travelled fifty thousand miles, a great deal of it on foot. They called him "Mr. Astronomer" Thompson and said that he was such a vivid storyteller that when he described a snow storm you could close your eyes and feel the cold flakes on your cheeks!

On the one hundredth anniversary of his death, June 5, 1957, Canada issued a five-cent ultramarine stamp showing Thompson with his sextant and a great map of the Western Canada which he did so much to reveal.

Settlement

The settlement of Canada and the growth of population were rather slow before the nineteenth century. This was due in part to the concentration on fish and furs by the early English and French adventurers who either came as explorers themselves or followed on the paths the explorers had marked out.

The first English settlement was in Newfoundland. The island and its fisheries by the early seventeenth century were an old story to the merchants of Bristol. More than a hundred years had passed since John Cabot's famous voyage, and it seemed to an energetic Bristol politician named John Guy to be time something more was done than just sending a fishing fleet to Newfoundland every year.

Guy had been sheriff of Bristol and had a finger in many of the city's biggest commercial organizations. He visited Newfoundland in 1608, the year Champlain was founding Quebec, and wrote an account of what he had seen. He argued that there should be an English settlement there.

In 1610 Guy and some associates, men of means from the two cities, formed the London and Bristol Company to which James I gave a charter granting it the whole island but with special emphasis on the Avalon Peninsula. Guy was made governor and set out with a group of settlers on July 5, 1610. He chose a site on a cove in Conception Bay for his little town, now known as Cupids, though in Guy's day it was called Cuper's Cove. The first winter was a mild one, the settlers worked hard at building and fortifying their new home and the venture seemed to be off to a good start.

Guy went home in 1611 and returned the next year with more colonists, and now troubles began to develop. The pirate, Peter Easton, arrived on the Newfoundland coast that year "with ten sayle of good ships well furnished and very rich," made Harbour Grace his headquarters and proceeded to raid and harry fishing fleets and their shore establishments at his leisure. Guy spent some time with Easton and apparently persuaded him not to bother the colony. Perhaps because he was

Two 1910 Newfoundland stamps — the three-cent John Guy and the two-cent Arms of the London and Bristol Company.

anxious to obtain a royal pardon, Easton spared Cuper's Cove, although one of the colonists was shot by mistake and the colony, willingly or not, presented the pirate with two pigs.

Guy was busy with other things at home, becoming mayor of Bristol in 1618, and at the same time his interest in the London and Bristol Company declined. He left Newfoundland, probably for the last time, in 1614. The colony then had sixty inhabitants, both men and women, and seemed likely to succeed. Guy went on to be a very active member of Parliament, still retaining an interest in the welfare of Newfoundland and speaking in the House of Commons in support of measures likely to be of benefit to the colonists and the fishermen. Easton, the pirate, never got his pardon, though one was issued. He was given shelter by the Duke of Savoy who welcomed a man with treasure worth two million pounds in his possession. He even got a title, "Marquis of Savoy," married a very wealthy wife and may have lived happily ever after, though there is no record of him after 1620.

· · · · ·

John Guy was not the only Briton to see advantages in the establishment of a colony in America. Sir William Alexander, Earl of Stirling, was a Scots nobleman with an empty purse and a head simply buzzing with schemes that would, if they succeeded, bring him power and fill his purse to overflowing at the same time. He saw no good reason why there should not be Scottish colonies across the seas. Since he was well known to King James I because he had held various offices in and about the royal household, he approached the king with his plan and caught the royal imagination.

James, on September 10, 1619, made Alexander the lord proprietor of a territory considerably bigger than Scotland

The five-cent Arms of Nova Scotia, with mayflower (trailing arbutus), a 1964 issue.

itself. It included the present provinces of Nova Scotia, New Brunswick and Prince Edward Island, and the Gaspé Peninsula. It was New Scotland, or "Nova Scotia." Alexander's next problem was to find settlers and money with which to carry them to Nova Scotia and provide them with whatever they needed until the new colony became self-supporting. Once again the king provided the solution. Some years earlier he had instituted a new minor order of hereditary nobility — the knight baronet. He had literally sold this new title to country gentlemen who could be counted upon to support the king against those who opposed him. The purchaser became a "Sir" and his wife a "Lady" in return for which he paid £3000 into the Treasury. That this was a very considerable sum of money may be realized by the wage scale at the time. Labourers worked six days a week from daylight to dark for from four to five shilling a week. Skilled tradesmen were paid about sixpence more.

James had used funds raised in this way to pay for the settlement of English and Scottish settlers in Ulster. He now proposed to use the same method to pay for the settlement of Nova Scotia with the added attraction that each Baronet of Nova Scotia would be given a large grant of land in the new colony. In addition to paying for the title they would each have to provide six settlers, fully armed, and keep them clothed and provisioned in Nova Scotia for two years.

The result: nothing. Not a man came forward to take up the offer. James died without ever creating a Baronet of Nova Scotia or recruiting a single settler.

His son Charles I, at the urging of Sir William Alexander, was a little more successful. By 1626 twenty-eight candidates had come forward. Charles awarded armorial bearings to the province and it was from these that the arms of the Province of Nova Scotia and the provincial flag derived. As an added inducement the baronets were permitted to wear a personal decoration, a riband and badge, similar to the escutcheon or shield in the provincial coat of arms. This shield, in fact, is the National Arms of Scotland with the colours counter-changed, a blue Cross of St. Andrew on a silver or white field rather than the white cross on a blue field. The arms and the badge on its "orange-tawny Riband" brought in fifteen additional subscribers, and with this result the king and Alexander had to be content.

It was 1629 before any settlers crossed the Atlantic. In that year Sir William Alexander's son, also named William, built a fort and the beginnings of a settlement at Port-Royal where French colonists had been living more or less continuously for twenty-five years. Young William's friend Sir James Stewart, Lord Ochiltree, at the same time was setting up another fort at Baleine on Cape Breton Island. The French immediately swooped down on Ochiltree's little settlement and carried the inhabitants off to prison in France. Charles I was next faced with a dilemma. He could make peace with France and probably get his French wife's dowry, which had not been paid and which he needed desperately since he could not wring enough money out of Parliament to carry on the government. Or he could support Sir William Alexander's Port-Royal colony and probably lose the dowry. It was an easy decision. He recalled the Scots and signed the Treaty of St. Germain-en-Laye in 1632 returning New Scotland to France. One or two of the Scots remained to live with the French at Port-Royal, the others sailing home in the ship *Saint Jean*.

. . . . .

When Louis XIV ruled France he was assisted from time to time by very able men. One of the greatest of these was Jean Baptiste Colbert who, about 1601, became Louis' chief adviser on taxation, trade and industry, and commercial matters.

The five-cent Jean Talon presenting gifts to a young farm couple, issued in 1962.

Colbert had great plans to make France wealthy and powerful and he gained much success in the pursuit of these plans. At the time each province of France had an official, called the *intendant*, who reported to the king through one of the king's principal ministers. The intendant was a kind of supervisor, or general manager, with so many duties to perform that many of the intendants must have been worried and worn out in a very short time.

One of the successful ones was a young man named Jean Talon whose province was Hainault. When Colbert was looking for someone to take in hand the sadly tangled affairs of New France he chose Talon as the man most likely to make the colony play its part in his plan for the prosperity of France. So Jean Talon arrived at Quebec in the autumn of 1665 to serve, at his own request, for only two years as the intendant of New France.

He found the colony in very bad condition. The war with the Iroquois had been going on for twenty years, draining New France of the energy which should have been applied to other things. Because of this war, the fur trade, on which the life of the colony depended, had almost died out. The Company of One Hundred Associates, which had held the trading monopoly for many years, had lost interest and had recently been dissolved by the king who had replaced it with a new company designed by Colbert, the *Compagnie des Indes occidentales*. But the new company was only about a year old and had had no effect on colonial life and business.

Talon was appointed intendant of justice, police and finances in Canada, Acadia, Newfoundland and wherever else in North America France claimed ownership. He was expected to set up and supervise the law courts, to act as a judge in civil cases himself and to see that proper punishments were imposed on the guilty. He had to control the colony's money matters including the payment of soldiers stationed there. He was expected, in fact ordered, to develop the agriculture, industries and trade of the colony so that it would support itself and stop draining France of funds.

Talon served two terms as intendant of New France, a total of less than six years, but such was his energy and ability that he transformed the dying colony into a thriving and busy country. He brought out many colonists including the famous *filles du roi*, spinsters who came, with the certainty of marriage, to a land where there was an overabundance of healthy young men and very few women. He imported horses, cattle and sheep. He obliged the settlers to build ships, to grow hemp, make rope and tar with which to equip the ships. Men had caught fish, but Talon established a fishing industry and shipped cured fish to the West Indies and France. Disturbed by the quantity and the cost of brandy imported from France and used to bribe the Indians, a practice which offended the Church, he set up a brewery. Having pleased the clergy by his attitude on brandy supplied to Indians, he offended them by insisting that those who had been granted land put it to use in agriculture or lose it to someone who would. He had men search for minerals, built up trade between Canada and Acadia, and even sent a little coal from Cape Breton to France. He established a shoe factory which used the hides made available by the increase he had brought about in the number of cattle in the country, and this factory was soon producing up to eight thousand pairs of shoes a year. He built a tannery to supply the shoe factory with leather and, by setting up a hat factory at Quebec, made it possible to be dressed from top to toe in clothing produced in Canada. The looms he had had brought in were already supplying all the necessary kinds of cloth, from a coarse muslin to serge. His encouragement of the farmers to grow more wheat even posed a problem that Canada has not solved three hundred years later. There was soon a surplus of wheat and no easy way of selling it.

The ten-cent view of Quebec in 1700, issued in 1908.

Talon returned to France for good in 1672. With his departure the colony quickly ran down again. The rulers of France never had any really strong interest in Canada and only gave it their full attention for short periods, usually during a war. Voltaire probably spoke for the majority of Frenchmen when he dismissed the country as *quelques arpents de neige*, a few acres of snow. When he heard that Canada was lost he said that "being glacial deserts" perhaps it was not really a loss after all. Louis XIV did not appoint a successor to Talon for three years, and the work he had done was not continued. The industries closed, trade lapsed again and the great improvements he had brought about were allowed to wither away.

. . . . .

France and England were at war from 1689 to 1697. In North America it was a frontier war, a long series of savage raids on each other's settlements with no decisive or very important battles. But a measure of success of the colonizing skill of the two races may be found by comparing the populations. The growth of Canada was slow. There were one hundred thousand English colonials and about fifteen thousand French. Yet when peace came in 1697, there could be no doubt of the permanence of New France. The little capital, Quebec, had a population of about two thousand. Its important buildings, mainly churches and other religious structures, were being built of stone by the end of the seventeenth century.

The ten-cent dark violet stamp of the set issued in 1908 to mark Quebec's tercentenary shows a picture of the city in 1700. The spires of its churches rise above the houses, many of them stone, in which the merchants lived close to wharves and warehouses of the Lower Town.

The treaty of St. Germain-en-Laye, in 1632, ended a war between England and France and also ended Sir William Alexander's hopes for a Scottish colony in North America. Charles I gave him strict orders to withdraw all his people and their possessions. At the same time the French king chose Isaac de Razilly as his lieutenant general in New France and sent him to take possession of Port-Royal, in Acadia, and see that the Scots were sent packing.

De Razilly gave Port-Royal to his brother Claude de Razilly and himself took up residence at La Have where he set up a company to carry on the fisheries. By the time he died, four years later, he had brought forty families there and these people, who were later moved to Port-Royal, were the first substantial group of French colonists to be brought to Acadia and were the principal ancestors of the Acadians of today. Thirty years later there were 592 people at or near Port-Royal not counting thirty soldiers in the fort. As their numbers increased they opened new tracts of land to farming. They kept to the rich river bottoms and the salt marshes of the estuaries which they enclosed with dikes so that they provided great quantities of hay and autumn pasture for the growing herds of cattle. It is said they quarrelled readily over land, but this is common in pioneer communities lacking other forms of dramatic entertainment.

Neglected by France and despised by the Canadians, who for some not very obvious reason felt themselves to be superior to them, they became, after 1710 when Nova Scotia came into possession of the British, almost a race apart. Industrious, pious and good-humoured, they were content to live their lives in tune with the seasons — farming, fishing, trapping a little. They had all the virtues and defects of a peasant society. The *Canadiens* had a phrase, *entêté comme un Acadien*, that perhaps contained a little truth. Stubborn they were and averse from change. And change, though they did not realize it, was a condition of their lives as it is of ours.

They became caught between the contending forces of France and Britain. Successive English governors demanded that they take the oath of allegiance, after the fall of Port-Royal, on the accession of George I and George II, and on other occasions. They tried persuasion, they tried threats — Take the oath or leave the province. The Acadians shuffled, made conditions which were unacceptable, refused outright. Some even took the oath as required. When they prepared to leave as an alternative to taking it they were persuaded to stay.

France, represented by the authorities in Quebec, urged them to remember that they were French, suggested that their religion was in danger from the Protestant British, and threatened them with the dire penalties of Indian reprisals if they wavered in their loyalty to that distant King Louis in Versailles, busy with his mistresses and the rigidities of courtly protocol in a nation well down the slope into bankruptcy. Quebec reported to Paris that twenty-five hundred able-bodied Acadians could be enrolled in the army if required. Just before the end of the War of the Austrian Succession, when Coulon de Villiers with his mixed force of Canadians and Indians invaded the province, he was joined by a few adventurous young Acadians. They were present when Villiers surprised Colonel Noble and his New Englanders at Grand Pré one winter night and killed or captured about half the detachment. It was an incident New England did not forget.

Britain and France fought a series of wars that lasted the entire eighteenth century and beyond. One of these, the War of the Austrian Succession, (1744-1748), left France reasonably successful in Europe but disastrously defeated in America. A surprise of the war was the capture of the magnificent fort of Louisbourg (now Louisburg), in 1745, by a hastily organized and rather haphazard army of New England volunteers and a British naval squadron. The New Englanders were furious when, in the treaty ending the war, Louisbourg

The four-cent Founding of Halifax, 1749, issued in 1949.

was restored to France in exchange for Madras in India.

But though the British had given Louisbourg back they realized that Acadia, or Nova Scotia, was the area where in any future war they would have to fight the French. The time had come to strengthen their grasp on Nova Scotia which New Englanders had won for them in 1710 and which they had neglected ever since.

A serious effort was made to gather a body of settlers and to establish a town and fortifications on the magnificent Chebucto Harbour that would counterbalance Louisbourg, Settlers were promised free land — fifty acres for the head of a family and ten additional acres for each member of his family. In addition each settler got tools, supplies, farm implements and rations for a whole year. It was hoped that discharged soldiers and sailors would volunteer and that skilled men, carpenters, masons, smiths and other tradesmen would be attracted to join. There was a rush of volunteers but not very many of them were of the kind desired and needed in a new country. Cockneys from London's slums to whom the promise of a year's free food seemed like a glimpse into Paradise made up the majority of the volunteer settlers.

H.M.S. *Sphinx* carrying the new governor, Colonel the Honourable Edward Cornwallis, and his staff arrived in Chebucto, now Halifax, Harbour on June 21, 1749, a day that has been celebrated annually ever since. A few days later the transports arrived carrying 2,576 settlers, and a start was made at once to build the new town. It was decided to name the place after the king's minister responsible for its establishment, the president of the Board of Trade and Plantations. His name was singularly unmusical but fortunately he had a title. He was George Dunk, Earl of Halifax.

As for the rabble of settlers, they proved so unskilled, unwilling and listless that not enough shelters were built to house them before winter came again. Half or more of them remained crowded on the ships that had brought them from London. Ship fever — typhus — broke out among them as it was to do on immigrant ships for more than the next hundred years, and a thousand of the unhappy wretches died before Spring. Most of the others drifted away during the next few years to old established towns like Boston, New York or Philadelphia, and their places were taken in Halifax by people from the older American colonies, mainly from New England.

The scene shown on the commemorative stamp issued on June 21, 1949, the bicentenary of the arrival of Cornwallis, shows houses being erected while a sentry in full regimentals marches his beat, on guard against the unknown perils of a strange new land.

The design itself is copied from a drawing by the great historical artist, Charles W. Jefferys, O.S.A., R.C.A., LL.D. (1869-1951). Jefferys was an artist-historian who spent most of his long and busy life recording Canada's past. The firm, clean line of his art depicts in hundreds of drawings the characters and events that make up Canadian history.

. . . . .

Although the war had ended in 1748 both sides knew the peace would not last, and both sides, in America at least, began to prepare for the struggle to be renewed. When Halifax was founded the new governor, Cornwallis, demanded once more that the Acadians take the oath of allegiance, and the Acadians once more refused to take the oath unless it was qualified by a guarantee that they could remain neutral in the event of a war. They also said that if their condition was not met they would withdraw from the country. The governor refused them permission to leave, in spite of their plea that they were being threatened with harm if they did not do so. The coercion was being applied by La Corne, a French officer commanding a mixed force of French regulars, Canadian guerillas and Indians, who stationed himself at the Isthmus of Chignecto, and by Le Loutre who, in the guise of missionary priest to the Indians, stirred both them and some of the Acadians to acts of violence. Cornwallis replied by putting a price on Le Loutre's head and offering £10 for every Indian scalp brought in — besides using troops to hold strategic points and overawe the attackers.

This condition of guerrilla war continued and, in fact, became worse during the next few years. Elsewhere in America fighting was continuous. In the Ohio Valley in 1754 Major George Washington of Virginia was fighting pitched battles against French detachments found in that disputed territory. It was almost as though the war, supposed to have ended in treaty in 1748, had never stopped.

In the meantime the government of Nova Scotia had fallen into the hands of a regular soldier, Colonel Charles Lawrence, who was acting governor while Hopson, who had succeeded Cornwallis, was in England on sick leave. Lawrence joined William Shirley, the governor of Massachusetts, in preparation for an attack on the French Fort Beauséjour at Chignecto. It was 1755, and full scale war became a matter of weeks or days. General Braddock arrived from England to be commander-in-chief in America. Plans were made to attack the French in the Ohio Valley, at Niagara and in Nova Scotia, and on June 16 Colonel Monckton completed his successful siege of Fort Beauséjour and accepted the surrender of its garrison.

It was at this time that Colonel Lawrence and his council decided that stern measures would have to be taken against the Acadians who still refused allegiance to the British king, asking to be allowed to live a separate life as neutrals. The plan was made to gather them up and send them out of the province, scattering them among the British colonies along

The fifty-cent Grand Pré Memorial Park, with Evangeline monument, issued in 1930.

the Atlantic coast. There is evidence that this plan had already been discussed with Governor Shirley of Massachusetts, whose idea it may have been, and at about this time Lawrence got a letter from Shirley's deputy suggesting that the time had come to remove these people — "What confidence can be placed in subjects who are inclined to revolt whenever they can do it with safety?"

Boston agreed to provide the transport to carry the Acadians away and the troops to undertake their capture and guard them until they embarked. Lawrence reported to London on July 18 what he had planned, and on September 2 the Acadians were ordered to assemble at various points in the province where the New England troops could guard them until the ships arrived to take them away.

At Grand Pré, all the men, ten years old and upwards, were ordered to gather in the church. When over four hundred of them arrived, Colonel Winslow of Massachusetts told them that their goods and lands were forfeited to the king and that he had orders, which he would obey, to remove them from the province. He promised, and later carried out the promise, that families would not be divided and that they could take their money and household goods with them — what they could carry in fact. Five days later the prisoners, their wives and children, a total of 1,923 people, were placed upon the ships bound for North Carolina, Virginia and Maryland.

Similar scenes took place at Annapolis Royal, Fort Cumberland, and other places. The smoke of burning farms stained the clear autumn skies as the transports came and went. It was winter before the operation was completed, the last transport leaving Minas Basin about a week before Christmas. Estimates of the number of people exiled in 1755 range from the ridiculously low figure of "a few hundred families," to the probable over-estimate of ten thousand. Perhaps six thousand to sixty-five hundred may be a more reliable figure. Many Acadians escaped to Cape Breton or to parts of New Brunswick occupied by French or Canadian troops. Some hid in woods close to their villages until forced out by hunger and winter's cold.

Lawrence had been very late in warning the British government of his intention to exile the Acadians. By the time his dispatch reached London his plans were complete. The secretary of state wrote back saying that Lawrence's intentions were not clear, whether he planned to expel only some of the Acadians who had taken up arms or all of them living in Nova Scotia. In either case the British government disapproved and gave its reasons. By the time the secretary's letter reached Halifax the expulsion had been begun and the Acadians had gone, scattered all up and down the continent. The majority of them found homes eventually in what is now the United States. Some escaped to the French West Indies and more to Quebec where they settled in L'Acadia, Becancourt and La Prairie. In 1766, after the war, nine hundred made their way overland to Nova Scotia. Strangers, the New England Planters, farmed the lands they once had owned and they made their way onwards to build new homes in western Nova Scotia.

The fifty-cent dull blue stamp issued in 1930 shows Grand Pré Memorial Park. The church shown in the picture is a replica of the Acadian Church of St. Charles in which John Winslow announced their coming exile to his prisoners. This is now a museum with a fine collection of Acadian relics. Before it stands a monument to Evangeline, the fictional heroine of Longfellow's poem.

. . . . .

The kind of government suitable for the colony of Nova Scotia

The 1958 five-cent stamp celebrating the bicentenary of Canada's first elected assembly.

was discussed in London in 1755 by the law officers of Parliament, the attorney general and the solicitor general. They gave it is their opinion that "the governor and council alone are not authorized by his majesty to make laws." Until there was an assembly, a legislature, laws for the colony would be made in London.

Lawrence, then acting as governor with a council of four, one of whom was the chief justice, was displeased by this decision. He and the earlier governors both at Halifax and earlier still at Annapolis Royal had passed laws that were necessary and the merchants and other people in the colony had never complained or suggested that he had no right to do so. Besides, he did not think very highly of an elected assembly. He felt it might serve only to "create heat, animosities and disunion." It might even include among its members "malevolent and ill-designing people."

Reluctant though he was, Lawrence was carried along toward the setting up of an assembly, a house of representatives. By January 1757 he and his council had drawn up a plan for the approval of the Lords of Trade and Plantations in London. It provided a house with twenty-two members which together with the governor and council would be called the General Assembly.

The plan with some slight alterations was approved in London and the election of the first representative government in Canada took place, the assembly being convened on October 2, 1758. Lawrence still had misgivings about how the elected members would behave. He wrote the Lords of Trade that he hoped none of the representatives would embarrass or obstruct his majesty's service, which makes him sound like a present-day cabinet minister at Ottawa trying to bully the Opposition. Nor were his fears entirely groundless. The members elected a Speaker, studied the revenues available to them and, as their first important act, decided to build a lighthouse. Having begun in this sedate, praiseworthy manner they suddenly turned on Lawrence's colleague on the council, the judge of admiralty, John Collier, and accused him to his face "with taking of such ffees [sic] as were grievous and oppressive, and such as the subject was unable to bear . . ." They followed up the attack by suggesting a bill to regulate the fees and brought up the thorny "conflict of interest" question by introducing a bill to exclude members of either council or assembly from employment under the government. It was rejected.

It had been a remarkable year. Not only had Nova Scotia elected its assembly, but the people of Halifax had seen what was to become a familiar sight in the years ahead — a great British fleet assembled in the harbour. Admiral Boscawen in his powerful ninety-gun flagship, H.M.S. *Namur*, with twenty-two other ships of the line and eighteen frigates, left Halifax convoying probably a hundred transports carrying Lord Jeffrey Amherst and Brigadier James Wolfe with more than twelve thousand troops. They were off to capture, for the last time, the great French fortress of Louisbourg. Lawrence went with them and it was his last military enterprise. Two years later, becoming overheated at a ball, he drank cold water, and this rash act, according to the ideas of the time, brought on a fever and inflamation of the lungs, of which he died.

On October 2, 1958, Canada celebrated the bicentenary of its first elected assembly by issuing a five-cent slate blue stamp showing the date 1758, a Speaker's chair and a mace.

. . . . .

On August 4, 1769, Prince Edward Island, destined to become the "Cradle of Confederation" and Canada's smallest province, was established as a separate British Colony. Prince

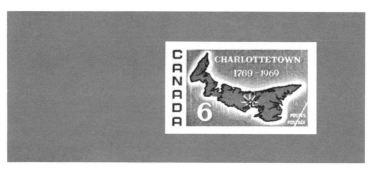

The six-cent map of Prince Edward Island, 1769-1969.

Edward Island is one hundred and thirty miles long and varies from three to thirty-three miles in width. In 1769 the total population was fewer than three hundred and yet it was given the complete official structure of a colonial government under the reign of George III. There was a governor, Walter Patterson, a lieutenant governor, a chief justice and judiciary, an executive council and a legislature. All the trappings customary in British colonies of the period were provided and the citizens had all the rights and privileges their fellow British subjects enjoyed in other colonies. The island was divided into sixty-seven townships which were distributed by lot to creditors of the British government each of whom undertook to place a settler on every lot of two hundred acres in his township.

There was little or no revenue. The governor, on arrival, had to build his own house and got no salary for five years, nor did his officials. The lieutenant governor very wisely stayed in England. The first Church of England clergyman quickly resigned, and the attorney general assumed his duties because he was deeply in debt and the minute income was welcome. The chief justice died, it is said, of an unlikely combination of starvation and gout.

As in larger, more heavily populated, provinces, Prince Edward Island saw the slow development from representative to responsible government. Its political history was tempestuous. Party rivalries were fierce, tenants rioted against landlords and the laws supporting landlords, while the local government was often at odds with the British government.

Prince Edward Island decided not to enter Confederation in 1867 even though Charlottetown had been the scene of the conference in 1864 when the delegates from Canada came to try to persuade the Maritime Provinces to enter into a union. It took the building of a railway, whose cost was beyond the colony's means and which drained it of both money and credit, to persuade Prince Edward Island to enter Canada as a province.

. . . . .

In the beginning the American Revolution was a civil war with Briton opposed to Briton. There were a great many people in Great Britain who supported the stand taken in the Thirteen Colonies in opposition to unjust taxes and the arbitrary use of power by the king and his advisers. In America itself there were likewise many people who opposed the actions of the British government but who believed, as did their friends in Britain, that a solution could be found that would satisfy the colonies without breaking the tie that bound them to the mother country. There were also, of course, people in the colonies who took the side of the king and his ministers just as there were in Britain.

The Declaration of Independence, July 4, 1776, put an abrupt end to any hope of a compromise or a peaceful solution of the dispute. Chatham, Burke, and their followers in England who supported the colonists, were at one stroke lumped in with King George III, Lord North and those who would suppress the colonists, as the enemies of freedom. Lord Chatham did not give up hope. Up to Burgoyne's disastrous defeat at Saratoga he made proposals that, had he been left to carry them out, might have brought America and Britain together again. But they were rejected at home and the tide of events in America had now risen too high to be reversed.

In America the effect of the Declaration of Independence was to divide Americans into two bitterly opposed camps. There could be no neutrals. Those who were not for unconditional independence were declared to be the enemy. The declaration had been made in the name of liberty, but the first acts under it deprived a large portion of the colonists, the Tories, of liberty of action and of freedom of thought and opinion. Tens of thousands of Americans were, by a single act of Congress, declared enemies, rebels and traitors because they would not renounce their allegiance to the king. Men who had been earnest advocates of colonial rights suddnly found themselves declared to be enemies of the colonies for whose rights they had contended.

Events in America fell into the pattern usual in revolutions. The extreme republicans, men who had professed to uphold liberty and to resist tyranny, now took tyranny as a weapon with which to deprive their fellow countrymen of liberty. Severe penalties, confiscation of property, imprisonment often under hideous conditions as in abandoned mines, banishment and even death were imposed on the Tories. A large minority of the inhabitants of the colonies — many of them wealthy merchants, landowners or professional men, others who were farmers, shopkeepers or tradesmen, either came from choice or were driven into the ranks of "the king's friends." One of them was Governor William Franklin of New Jersey, the son of Benjamin Franklin.

After Saratoga, France (and later Spain and Holland), hoping to profit by Britain's preoccupation in America and gain revenge for the defeats of the Seven Years' War, declared war on Britain. What had been a civil war between Britons now became an international conflict mainly between the age-old opponents, France and Great Britain. At Yorktown, Cornwallis surrendered to a Franco-American force in which the French considerably outnumbered the Americans and as well supplied the ships and artillery.

In London in 1782 the government headed by Lord North resigned and the king was obliged reluctantly to accept Lord Rockingham as prime minister and a cabinet that included many who from the beginning had opposed the war with America and who had urged that conciliation and a peaceful settlement be found. This new government acknowledged the independence of America and sought to bring the war to an end by opening negotiations with Benjamin Franklin, the American representative in Paris. A treaty was agreed to after a certain amount of bargaining. Franklin dropped his demand that Canada be given to the States and Britain was persuaded to allow Americans fishing rights off Newfoundland.

The question of the Loyalists, or Tories, was one of the most difficult to answer satisfactorily. At the beginning of the Revolution they had been the majority in colonies like New York and New Jersey and, if not a majority, at least a large minority in the Thirteen Colonies as a whole. By the end of the war their numbers had been greatly reduced. They had been plundered and scattered. Many had been imprisoned. Some had been murdered by lawless gangs posing as patriots and others had been executed by republican authorities. A considerable number had been killed in battles in which the Loyalist units like DeLancey's Brigade or the King's American Regiment had played their part. There was still, however, a large body of people who for whatever reason had remained loyal to Britain, and the British government tried to get them compensation. Franklin explained that nothing could be done for them by the United States because their property had been seized under the laws of the individual states, or former colonies, and that Congress had no power to force the states to return their estates or pay compensation. The best the British commissioners negotiating the Treaty of Paris could get was a promise that there would be no further confiscations or prosecutions and that Congress would recommend that the various states should give amnesty and restore their property to the Loyalists. This promise was completely empty, for Congress did not have the power, and perhaps not even the desire, to keep it. The state legislatures, one after another, passed laws against the Loyalists or refused to repeal such laws already in effect. Only South Carolina showed moderation.

There was nothing left for the Loyalists but to leave their country and leave it they did in their thousands. Some made their way to England from which their ancestors had come perhaps several generations before. Some from the southern states went to Florida, not then a part of the United States, or to the British West Indies. But most of them came to Canada, to Nova Scotia, to what is now New Brunswick, and to Prince Edward Island.

Sir Guy Carleton, the Irish soldier who had successfully defended Quebec against the Americans in their attempt to capture it in 1775, still held New York in 1782. To him flocked the Loyalists because, as one of them wrote, "No other resource for millions but to submit to the tyranny of exulting enemys or settle a new country." Agents for the Loyalists were sent to Nova Scotia to survey possible areas for settlement. They reached Annapolis Royal with an advance party of five hundred Loyalists on October 19, 1782. They visited Halifax and, crossing the Bay of Fundy, travelled up the Saint John River as far as Oromocto. They then returned to New York and the job of getting the Loyalists away began.

Carleton hired ships and organized the emigration. But Loyalists continued to reach New York as more and more of them learned that, as did Edward Winslow, soon to be one of the founders of New Brunswick, "The violence and malice of the Rebel Government against the Loyalists render it impossible ever to think of joining them again."

Instead of finishing in the Spring of 1783, as expected, the evacuation of the Loyalists went on until the end of November, with Carleton refusing to turn the port over to the new masters until the Loyalists were all safely away.

By that time thirty-five thousand Loyalists had left New York, mainly for Nova Scotia since the figures did not include those going to the West Indies or to Canada. Five transports filled with refugees sailed from New York around the coast of Nova Scotia and up the St. Lawrence to Sorel which they reached in the autumn of 1783. Their passengers continued their journey the following spring and reached their destination, Cataraqui (Kingston, Ontario) in July. Other bands of Loyalists followed the route north by way of Lake Champlain and the Richelieu River to Sorel or, turning west, reached Cornwall. Still others went up the Hudson River, thence up the Mohawk and, after portaging, by means of other small rivers, reached Lake Ontario, which they crossed to Kingston or the Bay of Quinte. A considerable number went westward along the southern shore of Lake Ontario to Niagara and Queenston or further to Chippawa and the country north of Lake Erie. Those from Pennsylvania and New Jersey made the journey on foot, carrying their children and what possessions they had kept. Many of these only survived because of the kindness and help of the Indians.

High taxes and high prices together with a debased currency and harsh regulations covering the purchase of land led a good many Americans to revise their opinions about living under a British government. Land was cheaper and easier to obtain in Canada and there was a steady drift northwards for fifteen years of people whom the real Loyalists half contemptuously referred to as "late Loyalists." Some, more brazen than the others, had even served in Washington's army.

Smallpox reduced their ranks while they were waiting for transport in New York. Ships were wrecked on the voyage to Nova Scotia and crews and passengers drowned. How many died along the trails leading north or in the first bitter winter in Nova Scotia and New Brunswick will never be known.

Those who survived took the British North American colonies along their first steps toward the formation of the Canadian nation. They represented all the professions, all the skilled trades. Many of their early hardships were due to their lack of experience in pioneer conditions, since a great many of them were townsmen. It was said, probably a little inaccurately, that immediately after the war there were more graduates of Harvard College in Nova Scotia than there were in

Massachusetts. In 1784 New Brunswick was made a colony separate from Nova Scotia as a result of demands by the Loyalists who had been settled there.

By 1791 the time had come for division of Canada into two colonies. A line a little west of Montreal to the Ottawa River, and up it to the Hudson's Bay Company's territory, divided the mainly French-speaking colony of Lower Canada from the mainly English-speaking one of Upper Canada. This left an English-speaking minority in Lower Canada and a French-speaking one scattered along the old fur trade route in the country of the Huron Missions of long ago.

In Upper Canada, as in New Brunswick and Nova Scotia, the Loyalists, who had come from colonies with a long experience of representative government and elected legislatures, took a leading part in politics, in the law and in business and cultural enterprises. Life was not easy. They had been given grants of land but much of it was still covered with forests. The British government, in an effort to help, issued food to them for their first years in the country. It was usually flour and pork and the new pioneers quickly tired of it. One of them in New Brunswick wrote to a friend, "We have nothing here but His Majesty's rotten pork and unbaked flour."

But these were the people who, together with French Canadians of similar courage and determination, laid the foundation of this country. The history of Upper Canada and the Maritime provinces for the next two generations is studded with Loyalist names and the descendants of these people are still to be found in Parliament, in the diplomatic service, on the bench and in the professions all across the nation.

In 1934 Canada issued two stamps celebrating the one hundred and fiftieth anniversary of the arrival of the Loyalists. One, issued on July 1, is a ten-cent green stamp bearing a picture of a family group inspired by the Loyalist monument in Hamilton, Ontario. On the stamp the central

The ten-cent Loyalist family group and the two-cent Seal of New Brunswick, both issued in 1934.

picture is flanked by two panels. In one of them stands Britannia and in the other an Indian wearing a feathered war bonnet and carrying a tomahawk. Each of these figures is surmounted by the old Union Jack carrying only two crosses, those of St. Andrew and St. George, the flag under which the Loyalists preferred to live. Each flag is surmounted by a crown. The other stamp, issued on August 16, commemorates the establishment of New Brunswick as a colony separate from Nova Scotia. It is a brown two-cent stamp showing the Great Seal of the province, presented to it by George III.

. . . . .

English-speaking Canadians when abroad are sometimes surprised to learn that they have been recognized as Canadians because their accent is "faintly Scottish." The arrival of a Canadian group at a joint meeting of Americans and Canadians in the United States was announced by the American chairman, "The oots and aboots are here!" And perhaps if some Canadians, even those lacking Scots ancestors, have acquired "faintly Scottish" accents it is not to be wondered at. For the late eighteenth and early nineteenth centuries saw the arrival in Canada of a great tide of Scots immigrants.

The defeat of Prince Charles Edward at Culloden in 1746 put an end to a way of life that had endured in the highlands of Scotland for ages. The clan system was broken up and the clansmen lost whatever claim they had to ownership of the land upon which they lived, and became the mere tenants of the chief. The highlands of Scotland are not good agricultural land nor were the clansmen of the eighteenth century very good farmers. The rents paid the chiefs, now become great landowners, were insufficient to produce the income required for them to maintain positions in society which they felt due to their rank. A way in which to increase income from their lands was to turn them into vast sheep-walks, and this meant that the crofters had to leave their little holdings and try to scrape a precarious living in growing cities and towns, like Glasgow, or leave Scotland altogether for lands across the seas.

The plight of the dispossessed Highlanders caught the attention of a wealthy and patriotic Scots peer, Thomas Douglas, Earl of Selkirk. His efforts to get the British government to provide assistance to Scots desiring to emigrate to the British colonies in America, to "give them homes under our own flag" so that they might "strengthen the empire," got a sympathetic hearing, but the government of the day had its hands full and had nothing to offer but good will. The war with Napoleon required every shilling and every ounce of effort Britain could muster, but the government agreed not to hamper Lord Selkirk in any plans he might see fit to undertake at his own expense for the assistance of the victims of the "Highland Clearances."

A wealthy man, Selkirk purchased eighty thousand acres of land on Prince Edward Island when the Hudson's Bay Company objected to his original scheme to take Scottish settlers into the area of the Great Lakes. Three ships brought about eight hundred people, the majority of them from the Isle of Skye, to Prince Edward Island in August 1803. The next year over a hundred more, this time mostly from Mull, were brought out to Montreal and thence via Kingston and Niagara to land near Lake St. Clair, the Baldoon Farm, in Upper Canada. The Skye Pioneers in Prince Edward Island have descendants there still, but invading Americans during the War of 1812 scattered the Baldoon settlers and destroyed the settlement.

Selkirk still had his mind fixed on the country south of Hudson Bay and west of the Great Lakes as a home for emigrants from the British Isles. The war with Napoleon gave him the opportunity he needed to carry out his plans. The Hudson's Bay Company was in trouble because the European market for its furs had been cut off by Napoleon, who was attempting to destroy Britain's trade. Selkirk was therefore able to acquire great numbers of Hudson's Bay Company shares at a comparatively low price and secured enough of them to give him effective control of the Company. He then had the Company grant him 116,000 square miles of territory in which to plant his colonies of immigrants. He had gained control of a great trading company and enough land to make him one of the world's largest landowners, but he had also acquired a resourceful, stubborn and bitter enemy — the North West Company of Montreal, the rival and competitor of the Hudson's Bay Company. The Nor'Westers had heard of Selkirk's plan to settle the West and they were determined to block it by fair means or foul.

Selkirk, meanwhile, pushed on with his plans. He got the best man he could find for governor of the new settlement, Miles Macdonell, a Loyalist veteran from the Mohawk Valley. His agents combed the Highlands and the Islands, the west of Ireland and the city of Glasgow for immigrants and, in 1811, three ships carrying this ill-assorted group of settlers left Britain bound for Hudson Bay whence the colonists would proceed to his new territory which he had called Assiniboia.

The expedition reached York Factory too late in the season to continue toward its destination and was obliged to spend the winter at this outpost on Hudson Bay. Macdonell found the settlers a difficult group to manage. When scurvy broke out one bull-headed Scot refused, in spite of the clear evidence that it was effective, to take the white spruce sap Macdonell prescribed as a remedy. When Macdonell, losing patience, locked him up in a specially built log jail, his friends burned it down and rescued him from the flames. The Glasgow men were shiftless and discontented, the Irish often drunk and spoiling for a fight.

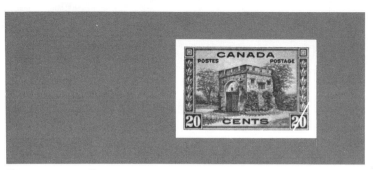

The twenty-cent Fort Garry Gate, issued in 1938.

It was midsummer before he got them, after an agonizingly hard journey in clumsy flat-bottomed boats they had built themselves, to the point on the Red River that was chosen as their permanent home. It was forty miles upstream from the mouth of the Red River to Point Douglas in the present city of Winnipeg. The date was August 20, 1812. Near at hand was the North West Company's post, Fort Gibraltar, and the Nor'Westers used it as a base from which to harry and bother the settlers. They sent the Métis to frighten the newcomers and tried to persuade the Indians to annoy them. Additional settlers came from Scotland in 1814 to join the struggling Red River Settlement where the farming had not progressed far enough to supply sufficient food, making it necessary for the immigrants to live on buffalo meat for months at a time.

By 1814 the Nor'Westers were taking active steps to break up the colony. Their agents managed by means of intrigue and clever lying to persuade some of the settlers to move to Canada and eventually used force. Macdonell unwisely agreed to surrender himself to the Nor'Westers provided they would leave the remaining colonists in peace. This was promised and the promise promptly broken. The colony was all but wiped out, the majority of the inhabitants scattered far and wide.

Selkirk had another lieutenant, Colin Robertson, a former servant of the North West Company, who refused to submit. He gathered up refugee settlers and led them back to try once more. Crops were now coming along in better fashion and the settlement began to show more promise. A new governor, Robert Semple, was appointed to rule the Hudson's Bay Company's trading posts as well as the colony on the Red River.

A courageous but short-sighted man, Semple could not understand the danger the colony was in, although he was

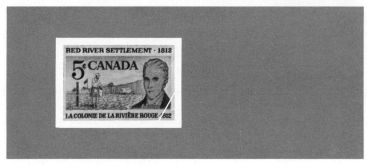

The five-cent Red River Settlement, issued in 1962.

warned repeatedly by Indians and friendly Canadians that the Nor'Westers meant to destroy it. Instead, he hastened the onset of trouble by having the Nor'Westers' Fort Gibraltar pulled down by a body of his men. On June 19, 1816, the Nor'Westers struck back. A large body of Métis and French Canadians, led by a Scots halfbreed named Duncan Grant, attacked the colony and, in what has been called the Seven Oaks Massacre, killed Semple and twenty-two others including most of the little band of troublesome Irishmen, the doctor, the governor's secretary and several of the leaders of the community. The survivors were driven away from the settlement.

Selkirk was already in Canada on the way west to try to save his Red River Settlement, and this time he relied on experienced soldiers rather than on peaceful crofters to defend the colony. There were two regiments, the De Meuron and the Watteville, in Canada where they had been sent a few years before to defend Canada against the American invaders. They were made up of men, largely Swiss, who were in British pay and who had been formed into units to fight the French. The Watteville regiment were veterans of Wellington's campaign in the Peninsula. Due to be disbanded, the officers and men of these regiments were offered grants of land by Selkirk in his Assiniboia territory, and a number of them accepted his offer.

Selkirk himself had been appointed a justice of the peace for Upper Canada and the Indian Territories. Armed with the authority of this office and accompanied by his veteran soldier-settlers he pushed on to the west where he turned the tables on the Nor'Westers by stopping at the North West Company's Fort William stronghold and placing the principal partners of the company who were present under arrest. Then he continued to the Red River to which the refugees of the year before had now returned. He pursuaded the Indian chiefs to sign a treaty surrendering their claims to land on either side of the Red River and then, leaving the settlement secure against its enemies for the first time since it had been founded, returned to Upper Canada where the courts were busy with lawsuits arising out of the violent events of the past several years. In 1818 he returned to Britain, his health undermined, and died in the south of France on April 8, 1820.

Two Canadian stamps recall his memory and that of the beginning of Winnipeg and the Province of Manitoba.

On May 3, 1962 a five-cent green and violet stamp was issued to commemorate the one hundred and fiftieth anniversary. It carries a portrait of Thomas Douglas, Lord Selkirk, against a pictorial background showing a kilted Highlander cultivating land outside a palisade. An earlier stamp, issued in 1938, is the twenty-cent red-brown stamp showing a picture of Fort Garry Gate, Fort Garry having been erected on the site of the Nor'Westers' Fort Gibraltar.

Government & Politics

Sir John A. Macdonald complained that Canada was a hard country to govern. He might have added that it had had a hard time gathering itself into a nation and reaching relative agreement on its constitution and form of government. When the Treaty of Paris in 1763 delivered the French colony of Canada into British hands, Nova Scotia had had an elected assembly for five years. One of the early actions (1759) of its members was to reject unanimously the proposal that they should be paid for their services — "They will not put their constituents to any charge for their attendance." Their successors in the elected bodies that govern this country soon got bravely over this state of mind, and one need not look further for proof that history does not, in fact, repeat itself.

The newly acquired colony of Canada was at first governed by a succession of military governors. These men were quite happy to govern without the assistance of an elected assembly. They saw much to admire in the French system of direct rule by a governor and council and they saw little to admire in an elected legislature where any Tom, Dick or Harry could get up on his legs and argue the wisdom of the governor's decisions.

The British and American merchants, who had come mainly as sutlers and army suppliers and who had remained as fur traders, were the people who asked for an assembly. Many of them came from the thirteen British colonies strung down the Atlantic coast and they had ideas that smacked of democracy, a form of political heresy the military men could not abide. So they advised against an assembly and the British government, willing for about the first, and almost certainly the last, time to pay attention to the views of the man on the spot, agreed with them.

The British Parliament in 1774 passed the Quebec Act. The "Magna Carta of the French-Canadian race." Among other things it guaranteed the free exercise of the Roman Catholic religion including the right to collect tithes and dues. A special oath for Roman Catholics enabled French Canadians to take part in their own government. They were, indeed, treated more generously and tolerantly in religious matters than were their co-religionists in the British Isles, being given privileges the Irish could not hope to share. The seigneurial system remained and so did French civil law. Canada was to be governed just about as it had been in the past, only subject now to the approval of authority that resided in London, not in Paris.

Except by the merchants of Montreal the Quebec Act was pretty well received. French landowners liked it save perhaps for the necessity to pay tithes, and the population as a whole had few complaints. The merchant class were unhappy not to have an assembly in which to state their views, but they were a minority and the governor could ignore them most of the time if not quite completely. When the American Revolution broke out the merchants of Quebec and the Americans who had settled thinly on the lands vacated by the Acadians in Nova Scotia were equally incapable of organizing a revolt or of joining the rebels in the other thirteen American colonies. They were too few in numbers even if they had had the will, and while some of them did sympathize with the revolutionists the majority were content to remain neutral.

The end of the war in 1783 was followed by the arrival in Nova Scotia and Canada of the Loyalists, and their coming altered the political picture. These were people who, though they were loyal to the Crown, had been accustomed to sharing in the government of the country in which they lived if only to the extent of voting in a town meeting. One of the first results was the partition of Nova Scotia, split in two in order that the Loyalists who had settled the valley of the Saint John River and the Passamaquoddy Bay area might govern themselves in a new province, New Brunswick. Halifax had been too far away and too disinterested to satisfy this large body of newcomers who were both frustrated and burning with a sense of injustice. The peninsula of Nova Scotia was populated with people from New England who, in the words of one of New Brunswick's new leaders "had been well-wishers in the late rebellion." Obviously men like Ebenezer Slocum, late of Rhode Island, who had seen his father killed on his own doorstep and his mother's ears hacked off by American "patriots" were unlikely to get along peaceably with the New England Planters of Nova Scotia whose sympathies possibly had been with the patriots. And yet in Nova Scotia itself they succeeded in doing so, though not without friction.

In 1791, the British parliament passed a new act, the Constitutional Act, one result of which was to divide Canada into two provinces much as Nova Scotia had been divided a few years before. The Ottawa River was the dividing line between Upper and Lower Canada, the former dominated by Loyalists who were, even by that time, probably a minority of the total population. Lower Canada had a bigger population, about one hundred thousand French and ten thousand British. Each province under the Act had a government under a lieutenant governor appointed by London, an appointed legislative council and an elected assembly. Upper Canada was given freehold tenure of land and British law while Lower Canada kept the seigneurial system and French civil law. The Roman Catholic Church remained the officially permitted church of Lower Canada. The Act preserved much of the old régime in Lower Canada and established a similar régime in Upper Canada with plenty of authority at the top and very little democracy below.

For nearly fifty years this was the system of government in the British North American colonies. In this time the population was growing. Land in Upper Canada was given to veterans of the Peninsular War and Waterloo. Thirty thousand Highland Scots came into Nova Scotia, and large numbers to Prince Edward Island and eastern New Brunswick.

The middle class was growing in numbers and in wealth and it became increasingly impatient with a governmental system in which the real power to make decisions remained with a British governor and an executive council chosen by him and appointed to office without any consideration for the opinions of the elected legislatures. Once appointed to the governor's council a member could only be removed by the governor himself, whatever the elected members of the assembly might think of him. Often enough it seemed as if the governors followed the policy used by the Duke of Wellington in the selection of his staff officers. Crusty and high-nosed as usual, the Duke had said that he, and he alone, would choose his officers and there would be "no nonsense about merit, either!"

However suitable this form of government might have been in the conditions that existed in 1791, it was less and less satisfactory as time went on. The growing number of people who disliked it found leaders to express their dislike and to organize an opposition to it. These spokesman, Joseph Howe in Nova Scotia, Louis-Joseph Papineau in Lower Canada and William Lyon Mackenzie in Upper Canada, all filled with zeal and all inclined to become immoderate as passion overtook their better judgement, were yet the men to whom the British North American colonies owed the introduction of responsible government. In the Canadas in 1837 there were actually armed rebellions. Unwisely begun and badly directed, the rebellions quickly flickered out when faced with the organized forces of the government. Papineau and Mackenzie both fled to the United States, where the latter, discarding the female costume in which he had escaped pursuit, attempted to persuade Americans to attack Canada until the American authorities, tiring of a trouble-maker, put him in jail. He and Papineau were eventually pardoned and returned home. In the Maritime provinces, matters did not reach the point of armed rebellion. Joe Howe, erratic though he often was and inclined to be carried away on the flood of his own oratory, was the son of a Loyalist. Loyalty to the throne and a passionate belief in the virtues of responsible government found equal merit in his eyes. Sometimes irresponsible and often foolhardy, he considered the actions of Mackenzie and Papineau foolhardy and irresponsible beyond reason.

The rebellion of 1837 brought Lord Durham to British North America in 1838 as governor general of the five colonies with orders to investigate the causes of the discontent that had erupted in armed rebellion and to recommend changes in colonial government that would prevent the repetition of such distressing occurrences. "Radical Jack" Durham, hot-tempered and hasty though he may have been, soon restored British ideas and practices to their old prestige. In five months of intense work he gathered the material for his famous *Report on the Affairs of British North America* that recommended responsible government. It was Durham's suggestion that the executive council be made responsible, not to the governor as in the past, but to the legislative assembly in each colony and that its members be chosen from the party with the majority in the assembly. It also recommended that all money bills be discussed and approved by the colonial assemblies. It further recommended that Upper and Lower Canada be reunited into a single legislative union.

When he returned home Durham was attacked in the House of Commons for exceeding his authority and promptly resigned. Some British politicians, including Lord John Russell, who was Secretary for the Colonies, had strong doubts about the wisdom of Durham's suggestions but, nevertheless, Parliament in 1841 passed the Act of Union which created the United Provinces of Canada. Upper Canada became Canada West and Lower Canada, Canada East. A legislative assembly of 84 elected members, 42 from each division, and a legislative council appointed by the governor, together with the governor, himself appointed by the British government and responsible to the Colonial Office in London, completed the governing structure.

This was not quite what reformers in the colonies had wanted. The executive council was still responsible to the governor and its members were appointed by the governor and held office as long as he wished them to. They were not dependent for office upon the will of a majority of the assembly. The legislative council, since it was appointed for life, resembled the House of Lords. Whether the system would work or not depended on the diplomatic skill of the governors. The first governor under the Act of Union was Lord Sydenham. He was determined to rule, to be his own prime minister. Against him stood the Reform parties, equally determined that the assembly should rule, that the council should be subordinate to it and that the executive should be responsible to the majority in the assembly. In the first Canadian Assembly, 1841, elected after the Act of Union, a united Reform party led by Robert Baldwin for Canada West and Louis-Hippolyte Lafontaine for Canada East stood ready to do battle with the governor.

Sydenham, however, died late in 1841 and was succeeded by Sir Charles Bagot, a diplomat who chose his executive council from the ranks of the Reformers and thus disarmed his critics. Baldwin and Lafontaine served under Bagot but found that they exercised no real influence on the government and therefore resigned.

In Nova Scotia the Reform party led by Joe Howe and James Boyle Uniacke had a similar experience. The governors could use their support but ignore their advice, a most discouraging state of affairs. An election in 1847 put Howe and Uniacke in the assembly with a majority of their followers. By this time the British government was ready to concede that the executive council should be responsible to the assembly, should become in fact the cabinet formed from elected members of the party holding the majority of seats in

The 1948 four-cent stamp celebrating a hundred years of responsible government in Canada.

the legislature. The governor of Nova Scotia, Sir John Harvey, on orders from the Colonial Office that the colonies were to have complete self-government in internal affairs, called upon Howe and Uniacke to form the first responsible government in any British colony, February 2, 1848. The change to responsible government in the other British North American colonies followed quickly.

The winning of responsible government is celebrated by two Canadian stamps. A twenty-cent dark red stamp carrying the portraits of Robert Baldwin and Sir Louis-Hippolyte Lafontaine was issued on June 29, 1927, rather inappropriately as part of the celebration of the sixtieth year of Canadian Confederation. On October 1, 1948, a four-cent gray stamp carrying a picture of the Parliament Buildings, Ottawa, the portraits of Queen Victoria and King George VI together with the dates 1848 and 1948, commemorates the centenary of the winning of responsible government. By some regrettable oversight Joseph Howe and J. B. Uniacke have never appeared on a Canadian stamp although as the leaders of the first responsible government they seem to deserve the recognition.

By 1855 all the British North American colonies had won responsible government, but political peace and efficient government were as far away as ever. Baldwin and Lafontaine had won the election in Canada in 1848 and before they resigned office in 1851 had, among other things, assumed control of the postal services that issued the red three-penny beaver stamp, Canada's first. But the united province proved to be an awkward creation. Representation in the assembly was not on the basis of population, so that Canada West had the same number of representatives as Canada East but a much larger population. The two language groups, English and French opposed and balanced one another, so that in order to form a gov-

The 1927 twenty-cent Baldwin and Lafontaine, and the five-cent Ottawa centenary as national capital, 1965.

ernment an overall majority was not enough. A majority had to be won in each division of the province. This resulted in confused and indecisive election results and a series of short-lived ministries under joint leadership — George Brown and A.-A. Dorion, John A. Macdonald and George-Etienne Cartier.

To the problems set by this political instability, the frequent impossibility of passing legislation because the "double majority" was not available, were added economic troubles arising out of the sometimes too optimistic construction of railroads, and the business depression following the loss of the British market when Britain adopted free trade. This last was so damaging to trade that the English-speaking merchants of Montreal openly sought annexation to the United States in 1849, a suggestion strongly opposed by the French, and getting no encouragement from the Americans.

The long and sometimes angry debate about the location of the capital was settled in 1857. There had not been a permanent meeting place for the Canadian legislature so that it met sometimes in Quebec and sometimes in Toronto. Quite apart from the inconvenience of this arrangement was the possibility it held for regional jealousy and strife. Queen Victoria was asked to make the decision the members of the legislature were unable to make for themselves and to choose Canada's capital city. The choice fell upon Ottawa.

Some time passed before anything farther was done but by 1860 construction of the Parliament Buildings was begun and the cornerstone of the main block was laid by the Prince of Wales, afterward King Edward VII. The first session of parliament in Ottawa was opened in 1865. This is recalled by the five-cent brown stamp issued in September 8, 1965, its hundredth anniversary.

There was danger, too, that the internal troubles of the colonies would be overshadowed by a growing threat from outside. The United States was growing fast and filling up the West with settlers. As the best arable land was taken up, American eyes turned to the north where the British North West Territories stretched, empty and inviting from the Red River to the Rockies. There were border disputes, too, over the boundary between Maine and New Brunswick and that between Oregon and British Columbia. The United States was led by ambitious men some of whom believed "the manifest destiny" of their country was to rule the continent from the North Pole to Central America. President Polk threatened war over the Oregon boundary dispute, and actually did go to war with Mexico in a successful effort to expand his country. The Civil War in the United States (1861-65) made matters worse since there was a good deal of sympathy in Great Britain for the Confederate States. The destructive raids on commerce by Confederate warships built in England angered many Americans to the point where they talked of seizing British provinces in North America in reprisal. There were raids into Canada after the end of the American Civil War by anti-British Irish-Americans many of whom had been soldiers in the Union army and who now called themselves Fenians. Not for the first, nor the last, time the British provinces were finding the United States an uncomfortable neighbour.

All these things gave renewed interest to a suggestion that had been made during Lord Durham's investigation of the political problems of the colonies after the rebellions of 1837. This had been the proposal that the colonies be united into a single country. It had not been practical at that time but now, with the new railroad lines extending east and west, barriers of distance between the colonies were disappearing.

Ten years after Durham's Report an organization called The British American League discussed the idea in Toronto and drew up a plan for confederation. In 1854, J. W. Johnstone, leader of the Conservative party of Nova Scotia, introduced a resolution into the legislature at Halifax that "Confederation of the British Provinces" take place and supported it with an eloquent speech filled with evidence and argument for the adoption of such a scheme. George Brown in his newspaper *The Globe* in Toronto urged that Rupert's Land and the North West Territories be taken over by Canada when the monopoly of the Hudson's Bay Company ended in a few years. Brown believed that Canada East and Canada West should form a federal union with representation in the assembly on a strict basis of population. Brown and his Clear Grit or Reform party were suspicious of the Catholic French, and representation by population would have guaranteed an English-speaking majority in the legislature. This suggestion was distasteful even to some members of his own party and, of course, quite unacceptable to the French. Some better idea was needed, and in the meantime the deadlock in Canada remained and approached a state of crisis.

In the Maritime Provinces new leaders had come forward, Samuel Leonard Tilley in New Brunswick and Dr. Charles Tupper in Nova Scotia. Tupper started his political career as a follower of J. W. Johnstone, who had been urging the union of the British colonies in North America since 1838. By 1860 Tupper was actively promoting the idea of a "re-union" of the Maritime Provinces and a federation of the five British provinces "to which ultimately the great Red River and the Saskatchewan country might be added." Joseph Howe, then leader of the government in Nova Scotia, gave his blessing to the idea of a union of the Maritime Provinces and in 1861 even introduced a half-hearted resolution that the possibilities of a wider union might be examined. He himself preferred that the North American colonies should elect members to the British House of Commons. But the next year Howe proposed that the colonies should have a formal discussion of the question of union. He asked consideration of the subject and suggested that if delegates were appointed it would "be convenient to have a meeting at some central place about

The three-cent 1917 Fathers of Confederation and the two-cent 1927 issue.

the middle of September." The invitation was not accepted. Howe was defeated in the election of 1863 and Tupper, now prime minister of Nova Scotia, feeling that there was no prospect of a large union, called in 1864 for a union of the Maritime Provinces, and a conference was arranged to meet in Charlottetown in September.

Before the conference met, the governor general asked the governors of the Maritime Provinces if the conference would receive a delegation from Canada who wished to give their views on the possibility of a larger union. He got a favourable reply, and a large group of Canadians made up of members of the legislature, newspaper men, business men and others interested in confederation promptly decended upon the Maritime Provinces. D'Arcy McGee was one of the group, who visited various towns in the Maritime Provinces stirring up interest in Canada amongst the people, to whom it was a rather remote and foreign country not nearly as well known as the United States.

When the conference opened in Charlottetown the strong delegation from Canada which included John A. Macdonald, George Brown, George-Etienne Cartier and D'Arcy McGee, made a strong plea for a political union of all the provinces. It was decided that a new conference should be convened at Quebec in October to discuss confederation of all the provinces. The Canadian delegation then visited Halifax and Fredericton, where they were entertained in the lavish Victorian manner with enormous banquets and oratory that made rafters ring with high-flown eloquence. It was at these meetings nevertheless that the first seeds of Canadian national sentiment were planted.

The Quebec Conference opened on October 10 in the Parliament Buildings of Canada East with G.-E. Cartier, attorney general for Canada East, as the elected chairman.

When John A. Macdonald, then attorney general for Canada West, made a moving and brilliant address on the advantages, indeed the necessity, of a federal union he was speaking to listeners most of whom were ready to agree with every syllable. The Conference in the space of seventeen days drew up a list of seventy-two resolutions which were to become the bricks out of which the Canadian constitution was built. There were thirty-three delegates (the Fathers of Confederation) representing different interests, races and religious beliefs. That they accomplished anything is a matter for some astonishment, but that they succeeded in setting forth such a long list of proposals that were, on the whole, so sensible and appropriate for conditions in British North America at the time was a most remarkable feat. It was not brought to pass without hotly disputed argument, and the leaders, notably the genial but very astute Macdonald, had to use the greatest diplomatic skills to keep the discussions productive of light rather than heat. It was intended that the resolutions be submitted to the individual provinces for approval and to the Colonial Office in London for both approval and authorization.

In Canada there was some opposition to the resolutions but it was mainly from small extremist wings of the Reformist (later Liberal) party. Newfoundland, whose trade ties with Britain were very close and which seemed to have nothing to gain by the construction of railroads connecting Atlantic ports with the Canadian hinterland, turned its back on confederation for seventy-five years. Prince Edward Island also rejected it, but for less than a decade.

It was in New Brunswick and Nova Scotia that the tempest of opposition was loosed. Forgotten were the cheering crowds that had lined the Saint John docks to welcome the newsmen, legislators and others who had made up the party visiting the provinces just before the Charlottetown Conference. Forgotten were the enthusiasm and good will that greeted the reports of the forthcoming Quebec Conference only a few

Sir Charles Tupper (1971), and George Brown and the Globe *(1969), both five-cent stamps.*

weeks earlier. In New Brunswick Tilley and the confederationists were defeated to a man in an election. In Nova Scotia the Liberal party opposed confederation under the urging of William Annand, owner of the Halifax *Morning Chronicle*. Tupper set up a system of free schools supported by taxation in 1865 and gave his political enemies another stick with which to beat him. Joe Howe, who seemed to combine within his personality two men, a great one and a petty one, admitted privately that where confederation was concerned "I will not play second fiddle to that damned Tupper." He had put himself at the head of the anti-confederation movement. Thus the man and the party that opposed free education and had re-imposed, a few years before, a property qualification on voters by revoking the manhood suffrage act passed by Johnstone and Tupper, now stood firm against another change — Confederation.

Our Victorian ancestors were hearty people with more robust appetites than we their puny descendants, now hedged about with the dire prophecies of food and drug authorities, of dietitians, of moralists, ecologists and other prophets of doom. Whiskey was cheap and plentiful. There was an abundance of hearty food. The conferences at Charlottetown and Quebec had each had its quota of banquets, balls and drawing rooms. Now the opponents of the Quebec Resolutions, those who feared and opposed the federal union of the provinces, indulged in language of denunciation that, too, was as excessive and violent as were other emotions of the Victorians when released after being long pent up. The "Botheration Scheme" was the mildest name Annand's paper chose to call it. The balls and banquets attended by the delegates were described by some of the papers and speakers opposed to confederation in terms that would have been exaggerated had they been applied to Roman orgies in the decadent days of

The 1927 one-cent Sir John A. Macdonald, five-cent D'Arcy McGee and ten-cent Sir George-Étienne Cartier.

the Empire's decline. Howe's supporters, angered by the prospect of paying taxes for the maintenance of public schools, burned some of the new schoolhouses, and their anger at the man who favoured both confederation and free education burned even brighter. Annand expressed the hope that fifty thousand Fenians would cross the border from the United States into Canada. "That would settle this Confederation business." Charges and countercharges of treason, bribery and assorted criminal acts filled the air, for this was a time in politics when almost no one hesitated to substitute personal attack on an opponent for reasoned rebuttal of his argument.

While New Brunswick was governed by anti-confederates that province was a barrier between Nova Scotia and Canada and there was little that Tupper could do to further the cause of confederation as long as the barrier stood. As it happened, the anti-confederate government of New Brunswick was badly led, divided and generally inept. It counted heavily on closer trade relations with the United States, and when the British North American leaders approached Washington in 1866 with a request for a reciprocal free trade treaty they were badly snubbed by a contemptuous offer from the Americans. In return for giving the Americans access to inshore fisheries they could have free trade in rags, firewood, unground gypsum, unfinished grindstones and unwrought millstones. Deprived of an American market as an alternative to confederation, Smith, the New Brunswick prime minister, was persuaded to resign. In the election that followed, Tilley, his campaign financed by Canadian money and supported by discreet British appeals to the Loyalist tradition of the province, won a complete victory. The road to confederation was open once more.

The Canadians had already appealed to the Colonial Office in London for support for confederation — Macdonald, Brown, Cartier and A. T. Galt having gone to London to

The Charlottetown Conference and the Quebec Conference — both five-cent stamps issued in 1964.

present their views in person. The governors of the provinces, under instruction from the Colonial Office, made known that confederation was favoured by the British government. Tupper now asked the governor of Nova Scotia to arrange that a delegation from each province, counting Canada East and Canada West as separate provinces, might meet with the British government and draw up a scheme of union that would assure justice for each of the provinces and protection for their rights and interests.

Sixteen delegates from the four provinces, counting Canada as two, met representatives of the British government in London in December 1866 and hammered out the framework of the British North America Act which established the Dominion of Canada on July 1, 1867. It gave Canada the constitution which, modified slightly from time to time, remains, over a hundred years later, the established form of our government.

This form of government is a monarchy. Macdonald wanted the new country called the Kingdom of Canada, but the British, sharply aware of the touchy and truculent state of American nerves in this post-Civil War period, preferred to avoid any possible cause for offense. Aware, too, that as the United States had just demonstrated by the Civil War it was advisable to have a strong central government and provinces with limited and clearly stated powers and functions, those who framed the Act gave the federal parliament power "to make laws for the peace, welfare and good government of the federated provinces."

The government of Canada closely resembles that of Great Britain with the executive responsible to Parliament and able to rule only as long as it can command the support of a majority of the House of Commons; and with the ministers chosen from among the elected members of that House. So

The 1935 thirteen-cent Charlottetown Conference, and the 1928 one-dollar Parliament Buildings.

Canada remains the only monarchy in the two Americas. All the other fully independent states are republics, all have fought civil wars, some of them over and over again and most of them have suffered and some still suffer under dictatorships. The flexibility, the continuity of the Crown as the symbol of nation outside the arena of partisan conflict, and the very real force of tradition, have given Canada a stability that no other form of government could have provided. With our regional interests, our diversity in race, religion and culture we have needed the focus which the monarchical form of parliamentary government has supplied.

Whether this will remain true in the future no one can tell. Changing conditions bring their own problems and the answers to them. Not all Canadians are completely satisfied with the present structure of our government. Some do not place any value on tradition as one of the threads in our national fabric, others are impatient with the delays that occur when Parliament debates proposed changes in the laws. There are those who want a stronger central government and those equally sure the central government should be weakened and the provincial governments strengthened. Changes have slowly taken place in the time, now more than a century, that Canada has existed; and on the whole our form of government has served us well — better in fact than those, for example, of France, Germany and Italy all of which have changed theirs several times since 1867.

The political growth of the nation is plentifully illustrated in our stamps. To celebrate the fiftieth anniversary of Confederation, Canada, then heavily engaged in the First World War, issued in September 15, 1917, the three-cent brown stamp which reproduces the painting by Robert Harris entitled *Fathers of Confederation*. It shows the delegates at the Quebec Conference but for reasons of design the picture

The five-cent London Conference, 1966 issue.

was cropped. There were thirty-three Fathers at Quebec but eight of them, seven at the right and one at the left of the original painting, do not appear on the stamp. Harris's painting, unfortunately, was destroyed in the fire that burned the Parliament Building on February 3, 1916.

Ten years later a whole series of stamps were issued to mark the sixtieth anniversary of Confederation. Once more Harris's *Fathers of Confederation* appeared, this time as a two-cent green stamp. The design of the stamp was changed, too, to permit the seven Fathers at the right of the picture to appear. Two of the architects of Confederation were also celebrated in this series. Sir John A. Macdonald appeared on the one-cent orange stamp issued on June 29 and again on a twelve-cent stamp which he shares with Sir Wilfred Laurier. There must have been good reasons, though they do not jump to the eye, why Laurier appeared on stamps celebrating Confederation, which took place when he was twenty-six and had not yet entered politics. He also had a stamp of his own, the five-cent violet, issued at the same time. Sir George-Etienne Cartier, who might have been expected to share a stamp with Macdonald, did not appear on one until September 30, 1931, when his portrait was put on a ten-cent dark green stamp.

The other authentic Father of Confederation shown in the series is Thomas D'Arcy McGee, whose portrait is on a five-cent violet stamp. McGee was a journalist and orator who gave his very great talents to the promotion of the idea of union of the provinces. Born at Carlingford, County Louth, on April 13, 1825, he emigrated as a very young man to the United States but quickly returned to Ireland where he edited periodicals, among them the *Nation*, organ of the Young Ireland movement. His association with this revolutionary group made Ireland too dangerous a place for him and he once more went to the United States where he founded and edited several Irish newspapers. In 1857 he came to Montreal and was elected to the legislature the next year. From then onwards he was a passionate advocate of Confederation and was prominent at both the Charlottetown and Quebec Conferences. He was assassinated at Ottawa by a Fenian on April 7, 1868.

Sir Charles Tupper and George Brown, two of the other most important founders of modern Canada, also had to wait some years before they appeared on stamps. Tupper's portrait is on a five-cent ultramarine stamp issued on November 8, 1965. Brown's stamp was even later, not being issued until 1969. It is a five-cent multicoloured stamp carrying the portrait of the Scots newspaper owner and leader of the Reform party, "The Clear Grits," who set aside his intense dislike for Sir John A. Macdonald to form a coalition government with him to govern the old colony of Canada and who joined with him to bring about Confederation and the new Dominion. Brown's portrait is shown against a background that shows his newspaper, *The Globe* and the facade of the Legislative Building at Charlottetown.

The Quebec Conference had appeared twice on stamps and the Charlottetown Conference, where it all began, was remembered in 1935. On June 1 of that year a series of stamps was issued that included a thirteen-cent violet stamp that shows the delegates grouped before the Legislative Building in Charlottetown. In 1964 two additional stamps appeared to commemorate the hundredth anniversary of these founding conferences at Charlottetown and Quebec. One, a five-cent black stamp issued on July 29, pictures the Confederation Memorial opened that year and includes the old Legislative Building as well. The other, which appeared on September 9, is a five-cent dark brown and rose stamp showing a single maple leaf and a hand holding a rather unlikely quill pen. On May 26, 1966, a five-cent red-brown stamp was issued for the hundredth anniversary of the London Conference. On it the top-hatted delegation from the North American colonies stands against a background of the Thames and the Parliament Houses at Westminster.

Expansion

Médard Chouart des Groseilliers and his brother-in-law Pierre-Esprit Radisson, a younger man, were a self-reliant pair of fur-trader-explorers with a sharp eye for profits and a strong dislike for official pomp and fussiness. In 1659 they left Canada to seek furs in the country west and south of Hudson Bay. The governor of New France was opposed to the expedition unless one of his officials went along, but Groseilliers made a blunt refusal and the expedition slipped away unsupervised.

Just where they did go is uncertain because Radisson, who wrote the account, was deliberately misleading and later probably doctored his story to make out a case for himself. There is strong doubt that they reached Hudson Bay and very good evidence that they spent some time south of Lake Superior. But, wherever they had been, they returned to Canada with a very rich cargo of furs, enough to bring a measure of recovery to the near-bankrupt colony. The governor, still stung by their disobedience, showed his gratitude by seizing the furs and fining the fur-traders. Radisson reported that he even threw Groseilliers into jail.

It was an expensive exercise of authority. Groseilliers and Radisson went over to the English who, with heavy-handed humour, nicknamed them Mr. Gooseberries and Mr. Radishes. Perhaps this was just one more example of good will toward them, for they quickly got backing for their scheme to sail into Hudson Bay to tap the vast resources of fur contained in the country around it. In 1668 two small vessels left England carrying the brothers-in-law to the Bay. Grosseilliers sailed in the *Nonsuch*, commanded by a New Englander named Zachariah Gillam, while Radisson sailed in a naval ship provided by King Charles II. Radisson's ship was damaged and obliged to turn back but the *Nonsuch* came home in 1669 deep laden with her cargo of valuable furs. The evidence provided by the voyage of the *Nonsuch* was sufficient encouragement for its backers to set up a company to use Hudson Bay as a route to the riches of the West. In 1670 Charles II

The 1968 multicoloured stamp commemorating the voyage of the Nonsuch.

granted a charter to the Governor and Company of Adventurers of England Trading into Hudson's Bay, and as its first governor Charles appointed his cousin, Prince Rupert. For the next two hundred years the history of Canada west of the Bay and the Lakes was intertwined with the history of the HBC, and the multicoloured five-cent stamp issued in 1968 not only recalls the voyage of the *Nonsuch* but commemorates the first step taken to win the West for Britain. In the summer of 1970 a replica of the *Nonsuch*, built in Britain, was brought to Canada and sailed Canadian waters. It will have a permanent home in Winnipeg.

By the time of Confederation the Company had acquired overlordship of nearly half a continent, most of it empty of people except for the Indians whose principal source of food was the buffalo herds, already declining in numbers as the American West filled up and deprived them of their southern pasture. The Indian depended on the buffalo not only for food but for clothing, footwear, shelter and tools, and for centuries man and buffalo had shared the Great Plains without any significant change in population. The arrival of the white man and the white man's technology ended all that. The building of the Union Pacific Railway, which was completed in 1869, cut the buffalo herd in two and it also filled the American West with new settlers many of whom were commercial buffalo hunters who were not content to kill just for food and leather. These newcomers were prepared to kill every animal they could find and to work at the task from daylight until dark. They were interested mainly in the hides and eating only the choice morsels, left the rest of the carcass to rot under the prairie sun. "They lived like pigs and ate like kings."

No one knew or cared much about the balance of nature or the effect the disappearance of one species might have upon other species, including man. But there is evidence to show that there were Americans who understood quite well that the disappearance of the buffalo herd doomed the plains Indians. These people also believed, as fervently as they did the dicta of the Declaration of Independence, that the "only good Indian is a dead Indian." So as the slaughter of the buffalo continued and as the Indians of the United States, failing to find a Genghis Khan to unite and lead them, fought their hopeless wars against the U.S. Army, unrest and trouble stirred on the Canadian prairies as well.

At the time of Confederation there were probably fewer than twelve thousand people, exclusive of Indians, between the Red River and the Rockies. The greatest centre of population was along the Red River, but Winnipeg's population was only twenty-two hundred by 1873. A great many of the people in the territory were Métis, descendants of mixed marriages between Indians and whites, usually French.

The country south of the international boundary had filled up much more quickly and, while the population of states such as Minnesota was sparse by present-day standards, there were Americans there who considered the best lands to have been occupied and who confidently expected to acquire the relatively empty land north of the 49th parallel. The American practice of looking to Canada to replace domestic resources used up by spendthrift dissipation is not a phenomenon peculiar to the late twentieth century. There were Canadian renegades in Minnesota, too, who urged pressure to make the Red River Settlement "drop like a ripe plum" into American hands. This, too, is a continuing feature of Canadian life. Every American penetration into Canada whether it be economic, cultural or political is cheered on by Canadians who have something immediate to gain whether or not is it likely to benefit their country in the long run.

Canadian leaders like George Brown had been aware for years of American ambitions and he had used the *Globe* to argue for the acquisition of the West by Canada. So had one of his lieutenants in the Liberal party, William McDougall, whose paper the *North American* urged that the West be annexed if no other way seemed open. These views were known and unwelcome to most Westerners. There was a small group of Canadians in the West, too, newcomers from Canada West, or Ontario as it was to become on Confederation, who had their own newspaper, the *Nor'wester*, and who were loud and aggressive champions of annexation. Arrogant and bombastic, they antagonized the Westerners, particularly the Métis who saw in them the foes of their religion, language and way of life.

The British North America Act provided for the eventual admission of Rupert's Land and the North West Territories into the new Canadian confederation. One of the first important undertakings of the Canadian government was to start negotiations for the acquisition of these lands from the Hudson's Bay Company as inexpensively as possible. Canada's hopes of getting them free of charge on the grounds that the Company's charter had lapsed were dashed by the British Colonial Office which came down on the side of HBC. The Company's asking price of one million pounds cash was so far out of reach of the new and impoverished Dominion that the Colonial Office once more intervened and suggested that three hundred thousand pounds and land grants around the HBC posts might be a satisfactory solution. This was the arrangement unwillingly accepted by both sides. Britain gave Canada a loan to cover the cash payment, and transfer of ownership and control began.

While all these prolonged negotiations had been going on among the Hudson's Bay Company, the Dominion of Canada and the British Colonial Office no one had thought to pay much attention to the people living in the country that was changing ownership. No one really explained to the Métis of the Red River country what was involved and how it would

The red, white and blue portrait of Louis Riel issued in 1971.

affect them. Not that the Métis were alone in the information blackout. The Hudson's Bay Company did not even keep its own official, the governor of the Red River aware of what was happening.

The uneasiness felt by the Métis and even the whites at the lack of news was replaced by fear when parties of surveyors came in from Canada and began to divide the land, after the pattern copied by Canadians from the United States, into square townships divided into square sections. The Métis land pattern was like that of Quebec with a short front on the river which provided means of transportation, and a long narrow rectangle running back from the river. Some of the surveyors made matters worse by announcing that they intended to stay and make a fortune out of land speculation. The Métis decided that if their land titles were in danger, on top of everything else the new régime seemed to threaten, the time had come to take action. They needed a leader and they found him in Louis Riel.

Riel was born in St. Boniface in 1844, the son of a Métis leader who, some years earlier, had opposed the Hudson's Bay Company's efforts to maintain its monopoly of the fur trade. The younger Riel was at school in Montreal for a short time and was working in the United States when the trouble began on the Red River. He returned to join the Métis and lead their resistance and among his advisors were several Americans, one of them at least an agent of the United States government.

He and his followers stopped the survey and followed up by preventing William McDougall, the newly appointed governor, from entering the territory. That McDougall (well-known as an annexationist and responsible, as Canadian Minister of Works, for the surveyors and road builders whose coming had so disturbed the Métis) should have been made governor was a major mistake. That he should have arrived before the territory officially became Canadian was an even worse blunder.

Riel and his National Committee of Métis issued a List of Rights setting forth their demands which included the setting up of a legislature and guarantees for the continued use of their religion, language and "customs and usages." It was a fair and reasonable demand, but it had no softening effect on McDougall, who had issued, in error as it turned out, a statement that on December 1, 1869, he was the sole authority in Red River on behalf of Canada. December 1 was the date on which Canada was to take over Rupert's Land, but Ottawa had got word of the trouble on the Red River and had postponed the takeover. McDougall had not yet been informed of the change in plan, and tried to raise an armed force to overawe Riel. It failed and the Canadians who joined it were imprisoned in Fort Garry.

Riel next announced the formation of a provisional government complete with its own flag. The *Nor'wester* was suppressed and the Hudson's Bay Company's accounts and funds were seized. McDougall went back to Ottawa to face a reprimand from Sir John A. Macdonald, and the wily politician and Hudson's Bay Company man, Donald Smith (later Lord Strathcona), was sent in his place to pacify the Métis with promises. Smith did his best and won over most of Riel's followers but Riel himself remained doubtful.

It was now that the hotheads took charge of events. The Canadians who had rallied to McDougall's call to arms had either escaped or been released from prison. They took up arms again and in a scuffle at Kildonan two men were killed. Sixty Canadians were then re-arrested without much difficulty and Riel made a fatal mistake. To show, perhaps, that he would stand no more nonsense he singled out one of the prisoners, an Irishman, named Thomas Scott, who was violently and loudly opposed to Catholicism and the French-speaking

Métis, tried him, found him guilty of counter-revolution and had him shot.

The shots that killed the Orangeman, Scott, set up echoes that still sound faintly in Canadian politics, but to Ottawa in 1870 they sounded like the crack of doom. John A. Macdonald held quiet and discreet talks with a delegation from the Red River and reached a settlement that included many of the items on Riel's List of Rights. It was agreed, too, that a new province should be created and enter Confederation beside the original four. But while this was being accomplished the Orangemen of Ontario were demanding revenge for Scott's judicial murder and the French of Quebec were openly expressing admiration and support for Riel and the Métis. To appease Ontario, a military expedition was sent west "to restore order" and the troops, many of them sympathizers with Scott's friends, created disorder instead. It took all the tact and good sense of Colonel Garnet Wolseley, the army commander, and Sir Charles Tupper's friend and colleague, Adams Archibald, the new lieutenant governor, to prevent another and greater outbreak of violence. What did happen is that many of the Métis, like the Boers of South Africa in a somewhat similar situation, packed up their belongings and struck off into open spaces trying to put as much distance as possible between themselves and the authorities they distrusted and hated. Riel and some other leaders went into hiding and, in 1875, were pardoned provided they remained in banishment from Canada for five years.

In 1971, as part of the celebration of Manitoba's centennial as a province, Canada issued a red, white and blue six-cent stamp bearing the portrait of Louis Riel without whose Red River Rebellion Manitoba might not have achieved a measure of self-government for many years.

. . . . .

The long arm of the Hudson's Bay Company had reached out far beyond Rupert's Land and the North West Territories, to beyond the Rockies to the Pacific coast. Thompson's explorations in the Oregon country had revealed its enormous possibilities as a source for furs and the Company had not been slow to establish its posts there. The Americans, too, had reached the Pacific and John Jacob Astor's fur company was ready to compete with the HBC and cared very little for monopolies granted by the British government. In the boundary settlement made in 1818 it was agreed that the land beyond the Rockies should be open to all, but in the next twenty years American settlers, thrusting ever westwards, flooded into Oregon and set up a clamour for the United States government to proclaim it American territory.

The Hudson's Bay Company, alarmed at this development, attempted not very successfully to attract its own brand of settlers. The nearest source for colonists was the Red River and at the Company's urging twenty-one families left Red River and struggled across the prairies and through the Rockies to undertake farming in what is now the state of Washington. Their arrival only served to point up the Company's problem, for while they numbered about one hundred in all, American arrivals each year were approaching a thousand. The Hudson's Bay Company read the signs correctly. There was every reason to believe that the 49th parallel would become the boundary west of the Rockies just as it was east of them and that the logical boundary formed by the Columbia River would have to be abandoned. It moved its headquarters in 1843 to the southern tip of Vancouver Island and built Fort Victoria.

It was just in time. James Knox Polk was ambitious to become the eleventh president of the United States in the election of 1844 and his campaign slogan was "Fifty-four Forty or Fight!," a reference to 54°40' North which noisy expansionists like Polk thought should be the boundary of Oregon. Once elected, though he still favoured the more northerly limit Polk was not quite irresponsible enough to fight, and Congress, in 1846, accepted the 49th parallel as the Hudson's Bay Company had expected.

The boundary settlement should have removed the un-
certainty about the ownership of the land west of the Rockies
but if it did so the relief was a temporary one. By 1848
Oregon had become a territory and could look forward to
statehood; and its people, firm believers in the "manifest destiny" of the United States to gain possession of the entire
continent, began to cast greedy eyes on the empty reaches of
what is now called British Columbia. Many of them drifted
across the border and became squatters. The Company saw a
threat to continued British possession in this movement. Once
a sufficient number of these interlopers had established themselves they would call for, and get, the support of the United
States government in declaring the country American territory.
It was this tactic used so successfully in Texas that resulted in
the acquisition by the United States of the American south-
west.

The Company therefore approached the British government with a scheme for colonization of the Pacific coastal
territories. It would organize and pay for the settlement of
strategic areas in return for possession and control of the
whole territory. This was too ambitious for London to accept,
and the Company in 1849 was given Vancouver Island alone,
with the condition attached to the grant that if the colony was
not sufficiently developed Great Britain would take it back
and repay the Company's expenditures.

No agricultural settlers arrived for some time, but
miners, mostly from Scotland, came to mine the coal deposits
at the northern end of the island and at Nanaimo. Some of
these later turned to farming and also became the first to
ask that the Island become a British colony free of the Company's control. It was only when James Douglas, Chief Factor
of the Hudson's Bay Company west of the Rockies was appointed governor that Vancouver Island began to make progress. The Indians, who outnumbered the whites by thirty
to one, he kept under control by dispensing justice that was

swift and fair, and by organizing a small militia force to be called on if necessary. His real troubles began when gold was discovered in 1857 on the mainland.

The second half of the nineteenth century saw one gold rush after another in California, Australia, British Columbia, on the Witwatersrand in South Africa and, finally, the Klondike. They caused population shifts, the rise and fall of governments, contributed to a least one war and gave rise to a great body of myths and tall tales. They even made a few people wealthy. The British Columbia gold rush of 1858 was typical.

Everyone on Vancouver Island who could possibly get away, even seamen who deserted from ships in Victoria Harbour, made for the mainland and the gold strikes on the Fraser and Thompson rivers. Then the word reached California, and all the surplus miners left over from the California rush of 1849, together with all the riff-raff attracted to a gold strike, poured north. In addition there were prospectors and greenhorns from Canada, the British Isles, Europe and elsewhere until, by the middle of 1858, there were ten thousand hopefuls prospecting the Fraser. Behind them came the merchants and suppliers, the gamblers, the pedlars of liquor and vice and all the shady characters present on such occasions intent on getting a share of any wealth produced as long as no labour is involved.

To make sure the Americans on the gold fields did not try to get the country annexed by the United States, Douglas declared the mining areas Crown property and forced the miners to get licences from him. Some of the Americans found Indians working claims along the Fraser and, since the nineteenth century American seemed to be filled with hate for the Indians, they attempted to drive them away. The Indians stood on their rights and fought back with the result that there were dead Americans as well as Indians. Word of the disorders reached Douglas who gathered some volunteers and hurried to the scene to restore peace and order. He appointed law officers in each mining camp and established the rule of law. The British government now took the step of setting mainland British Columbia up as a crown colony and made Douglas governor. He asked for troops to defend the new colony and to maintain peace within it, if necessary, and got a detachment of the Royal Engineers.

At this point in time another gold rush developed when a great strike was reported further north in the Cariboo region. It was a wild and dangerous part of the country and only experienced woodsmen could travel it with any degree of comfort and safety. Nothing discouraged the gold seekers who scrambled up and down six-and seven-thousand-foot mountains, plunged into deep valleys filled with tangled, dark and dripping forests and crossed rocky gorges on shaky and dizzy bridges built, and forgotten, by Indians out of a few poles and a little rope or rawhide. Many died, but a few got through.

It was obvious that a road would have to be built so that supplies and equipment could reach the new mining camps. Douglas, never a man for half-measures, gave his orders. The road to the Cariboo would be a highway eighteen feet wide, all four hundred miles of it. The government, the miners and private contractors combined to build it and the Royal Engineers provided the skill to hang it along cliff sides, propped up on log cribbing, or to blast out ledges so that it could creep round the flanks of mountains. By 1864 it was completed at what seemed in those days the enormous cost of one million dollars.

As the gold fever abated many of those who had come to seek fortunes on the goldfields, or who had come as freighters and merchants, settled down on the land. The mining camps became towns and gold seekers drifted into other occupations. Among them were the survivors of an epic journey from Fort Garry undertaken by the Overlanders, some two hundred people, mostly from Canada but including Englishmen,

Europeans and even a few Australians. They crossed the plains with ninety-seven shrieking Red River carts and several score horses, oxen and cows. The journey across the prairies was slow and tiresome — the carts frequently getting bogged down in the heavily rutted trails — but not particularly dangerous. Real trouble began when they got into the mountains with supplies running low, autumn well advanced and the trail often blocked by fallen trees or rock slides.

They split up after reaching the upper part of the Fraser, some of them attempting to run the river in canoes or on rafts which they built. Some of these capsized or broke up, drowning their passengers and spilling provisions and tools. Part of the Overlanders got through to Fort George and thence to the Cariboo. Others went on foot to the Thompson where they built rafts to take them to Kamloops. More lives were lost and, as provisions ran out, the survivors were reduced to living on chipmunks and whatever other small animals they could shoot, together with a few potatoes dug from the ground near an Indian encampment all of whose inhabitants were found dead of smallpox. They struggled into Kamloops more than four months after leaving Fort Garry. By the time spring came much of the gloss had worn off the dream of wealth from gold, and the Overlanders scattered into different parts of British Columbia or left the country altogether; but their perilous journey added a page of romantic colour to the history of the West.

A year later there were signs that the gold of the Fraser and the Cariboo was beginning to run out. What remained would require expensive equipment to extract it and few could afford it. The boom the gold discoveries had created was now followed by a business depression. James Douglas's term as governor expired and the Colonial Office believed the time had come to reorganize the two colonies. It hoped to combine them into one, but this idea was rejected by the colonies, so each was given a legislature, a governor and all the trappings

A 1958 stamp celebrating British Columbia's centenary. Opposite page:
A 1962 issue marking the centenary of Victoria as an incorporated city.

of self-government. The economy of the two colonies continued to run down and, under pressure from the Colonial Office, they were persuaded to unite, in 1866, into a single colony with Victoria as the capital.

The suggestion was made that British Columbia should join the Canadian federation, but in 1867 Canada was a very distant place and there were people in British Columbia who pointed out that California was both nearer and more prosperous. By 1870, however, Canada, through the deal with the Hudson's Bay Company, had advanced to the Rockies and President Grant, a better soldier than a diplomat, was suggesting that a slice of British North America might compensate the United States for the losses of shipping caused by British-built, Confederate, commerce-raiding cruisers. The governor of British Columbia, Anthony Musgrave, believed confederation was necessary to keep the colony out of American clutches, and union with Canada was strongly urged by a forceful character named Amor de Cosmos.

It is fashionable to lament that Canadian history is drab and colourless. The charge is made, of course, by people possessed of too little knowledge, slight imagination and no sense of the ridiculous. No history can be dull when such eccentrics as Amor de Cosmos strut its stage. He was born in Windsor, Nova Scotia, with the indubitably common but frequently distinguished name of Smith and christened by uninspired parents with the given name of William. He made his way across the continent, it was said, in an American wagon train and later arrived in British Columbia, having acquired somewhere in his wanderings a new name that echoed, faintly it must be admitted, the glory of Greece and the grandeur of Rome — Amor de Cosmos, "Lover of the Universe."

In British Columbia he owned and edited a newspaper,

the *British Colonist* which he used as a medium for the distribution of his fiery opinions and as a reflection of his flamboyant personality. His love of the universe, it may be said in passing, stopped short of Chinese immigrants in British Columbia whose presence he deplored. In due course he became a member of the House of Commons and premier of British Columbia, proving perhaps that to be slightly bogus is no handicap in Canadian politics, and in 1870 he was a prime mover in the drive to take British Columbia into Confederation.

Knowing that Canada was eager to win British Columbia as a province and thus acquire a seacoast facing the Orient, British Columbia in 1871 put a fairly high price on its acceptance of union. There was no long haggling over terms. Canada readily agreed to take over the colony's considerable debt and to pay the new province a subsidy as well. British Columbia wanted a wagon road built across the Rockies to connect it with the rest of Canada. Eventually the British Columbians thought a railway might also be built. But Ottawa, warmed by the glow of having acquired a territory almost twice the size of France, optimistically promised a railway would be begun within two years and completed in ten. The promise so easily given in 1871 proved to be far more difficult to carry out than expected, but unlike similar easy promises given to Prince Edward Island in more recent times it was not broken. It resulted in the construction of one of the world's greatest railways, whose building required the performance of engineering skills unsurpassed anywhere at that time. For a raw young country with a population fewer than four million people (3,689,257 in 1871) to attempt such an undertaking was an example of national courage and self-confidence not often found in any country's history.

Scenes of British Columbia appear on Canadian stamps with some regularity. The spectacular beauty of the province demands and gets the recognition it deserves. A five-cent bluish-green stamp issued May 8, 1958, celebrates the

The Parliament Buildings, Victoria, issued in 1935. Opposite page: The Pacific coast Indian house and totem pole (1953).

centenary of British Columbia. Appropriately it is the picture of a gold prospector panning gravel as so many thousands did along the Fraser in 1858. On August 22, 1962, a stamp was produced to mark the centenary of Victoria as an incorporated city. It is a five-cent stamp showing the British Columbia Legislative Building in black (which is also shown on the fiftycent stamp issued June 1, 1935) over a reproduction in miniature of the rose-coloured tuppence ha'penny stamp issued in 1860 by the colonies of British Columbia and Vancouver Island. This stamp was issued both without and with perforations, but the former were never placed on sale so that, as a rarity, a good specimen will cost the collector $650 or more. The perforated stamp appears in two variations, one deep in colour and the other pale. Good copies of either variety may be obtained for considerably less, used for $50.00 to $60.00 and unused for anything up to half as much again. In 1865 Vancouver Island brought out an imperforated five-cent rose stamp which is a true rarity. If a good specimen can be found at all, its price would perhaps be over $5,000.

One other Canadian stamp has a bearing on the history of British Columbia. This is the one-dollar gray stamp issued in February 1953. It shows a Pacific coast Indian house and totem pole, a sight which must have been familiar to the Hudson's Bay Company men and officials who formed the white population of the colonies a century later.

. . . . .

With Manitoba organized as a province, (even though prematurely as a result of Louis Riel's resistance), and the admission of British Columbia to the Dominion, there still remained an empty empire to be organized and held. This was the great sweep of prairie, the ocean of grass, between Manitoba and the Rockies. There were the Indians and the small groups of Métis, it is true, but the steady advance of the

white man had already begun to destroy the way of life of these plains dwellers. As the slow tide of American settlement moved west one Indian nation after another was forced out of its usual range and pushed westward or northward to bring it into conflict with other tribes already worried by the decline of the buffalo herds, the aggressions of white hunters and the deadly effects of white man's diseases — as happened in 1870 when smallpox killed an estimated 15 per cent of the Indians north of the border.

The Canadian government, shaken by the recent events along the Red River, were sensitive to events likely to disturb the Indians or to threaten Canadian possession of the Territories. It was Sir John A. Macdonald's aim to fill up this empty land with settlers as quickly as possible. Such a policy went hand in hand with that which demanded the building of the transcontinental railways. But the immediate task was to try to keep the land at peace and to make sure that it remained in Canadian possession.

As usual, the challenge came from the south. Shrewd Yankee traders had begun to sell repeating rifles to the Blackfoot who used them effectively on their ancient enemies, the Plains Crees. Others, equally unscrupulous, had found a way to easy wealth by supplying the Indians with liquor. They called it whiskey and it began as a cheap and nasty form of that beverage, but they made it go farther by watering it and then restored its bite by adding red ink, tobacco juice or even diluted sulphuric acid — anything to turn it into "firewater."

These gentry had their headquarters in Montana, but they opened "branch offices" in Canadian territory, called them forts — Fort Whoop-Up, near the present site of Lethbridge, was possibly the most notorious — and insolently flew the Stars and Stripes above them. From debauching the Indians to murdering them was a short step. American wolf hunters also came into the territories although "hunter" is a misnomer since they did their "hunting" by leaving poisoned buffalo

The six-cent "golden spike" stamp (1970). Opposite page: The twelve-cent 1927 map of Canada.

carcasses out where the wolves — and the Indians' highly prized dogs — could get them, and then they picked up the dead wolves. A party of them had some horses stolen, or perhaps they had only strayed, and set out to find them and punish the thieves. They came upon a band of Indians encamped in the Cypress Hills on the Canadian side of the border and, persuading themselves that these were the guilty horse thieves, succeeded in killing at least thirty of them, some accounts say eighty, for the loss of one of their own party.

When the Canadian government was informed of what was going on in the West, and a full report was made by an official sent to find out at first-hand, it took immediate steps. Sir John A. Macdonald passed an Act of Parliament that established a force of mounted police whose task would be to maintain the authority of the Canadian government in the West and to enforce the law. Events in the United States had shown that the use of the army for these purposes was a bad policy. The cavalry created more problems than they solved, and tales of the brutal treatment of the Indians by hard-bitten cavalrymen horrified large sections of the American public. Final proof of the failure of the American method came in 1876 with the defeat and death of General George Custer by the Sioux on the Little Big Horn in Montana.

The original force of North West Mounted Police, much later to become the Royal Canadian Mounted Police, numbered only 150 men, almost immediately increased to 300. The idea that this tiny body of men, no matter how well-trained or how determined, could patrol and keep order in so vast an area might seem absurd. Each of them would have thousands of square miles to supervise, but the force was made up in the beginning mostly by experienced ex-soldiers of the British army. They were police, not soldiers, but they were organized and disciplined in a manner that was at least quasi-

military, and by a stroke of genius their uniform was the scarlet tunic of the British army and blue trousers with the wide yellow "cavalry stripe." Nothing more likely to impress the Indians could have been found. They had always been on friendly terms with the red-coated British soldiers and red, of course, was a magic colour, the colour of power and courage.

With the coming of the NWMP the whiskey traders and the wolf poisoners faded back across the border. The Indians, reassured that law and justice had arrived, proved not to be too difficult and the very fact that the Mounted Police were present was usually enough to keep the Queen's peace.

The coming of the Police marked the end of the old West, the West of the trappers, the buffalo and the buffalo hunters, and of the free, wild, roaming life of the plains Indians. Behind the Police came the railway and behind the railway would come the homesteaders to break up the prairie with their plows or run their cattle on the ranges once home to buffalo herds.

The first of the immigrants, a trickle that was to become a flood, reached Manitoba in 1874. These were the Mennonites from Russia and before the decade ended between seven and eight thousand of them had reached Manitoba where they farmed the open prairie. They were followed by Icelanders some of whom later went farther west. Into the Territories came settlers from Ontario who found land near the older centres such as the Police post at Fort McLeod.

The railway had had difficulties unforeseen when the carefree promise of completion within ten years was so cheerfully given. The muskeg country north of Lake Superior had presented engineering problems that almost ruined the whole project. But if the railroad, rails and all, sank in Lake Superior muskeg, so was money engulfed in the steadily rising costs of construction. By 1885 the financiers and the Canadian public were thoroughly discouraged and Macdonald was doubtful he could persuade Parliament to provide the company

The five-cent 50th anniversary of Alberta and Saskatchewan (1955) and the 1935 ten-cent RCMP.

with more funds. If it did not, the whole dream of a transcontinental railway, the promised link with British Columbia, would be in ruins and no one could foresee the utmost limits of the general collapse that would follow. The group building the railway, who were led by Donald Smith and his cousin George Stephen, took the name Canadian Pacific Railway Company in 1880 and quickly found a general manager who would drive hard to complete the line. He was an American, William Van Horne (afterwards Sir William) who said he would build five-hundred miles of track across the prairie in a summer — and did it. When, in spite of Van Horne's drive and energy the financial wells appeared to be drying up, Louis Riel unwittingly came to the rescue.

The Métis who had left Red River after Manitoba became a province had moved west and joined others of their race in scattered parts of the Northwest Territories, near Prince Albert, in the Qu'Appelle Valley, near Edmonton and at a few other places. Some of them were squatters without legal title to the land they occupied, others held lands along the rivers where they had repeated the pattern of long strip river lots traditional with Québecois and their Métis descendants. By 1885 they were in trouble again. The buffalo were gone. Once more the white settlers were advancing, preceeded as before by surveyors who divided the land into neat squares. The Métis protested to Ottawa but got little satisfaction and their fears that they would lose their lands were undiminished. They could never be completely satisfied because the clock could not be turned back and the conditions they loved be recalled. They were not alone in their distress, however, because a good many white settlers were equally enraged by the Dominion Land Acts that set forth which lands were available for homesteading and how title might be obtained and held.

So the Métis sent for Riel who was now an American citizen teaching school in Montana. And Riel came back to lead them once again; but he was not quite the Riel of 1870. The intervening years had been unkind. He had been in mental hospitals, but the sudden rages, the delusions of grandeur and the twisted belief that he was a religious leader, even having a divine mission to lead the Métis, indicated that the tendencies he had shown as a younger man had taken a firmer hold on his unstable mind. His character had suffered morally as well and he was prepared to accept a government bribe to pacify his followers. When it was not forthcoming he prepared to give up the legal and even praiseworthy agitation for self-government for the Territories as he had accomplished in Manitoba and try a *coup d'etat*. Up until this point he had had a considerable body of white supporters even though his talks with various Indian chiefs, such as the Cree chief Big Bear, made some of them nervous. They wanted reform but not at the cost of an Indian war.

When Riel proclaimed a provisional government and called on Superintendent Crozier of the Mounted Police to surrender Fort Carlton or face an attack by the Métis, he was, in fact, proclaiming a rebellion. Crozier impetuously moved out with a mixed force of police and volunteers to arrest Riel and his followers. Someone fired a shot and Crozier had to retreat, after a short battle, with ten dead and thirteen wounded. This was the "battle" of Duck Lake which opened Riel's rebellion.

Riel, whose judgment had been less than perfect fifteen years earlier on the Red River, took the Duck Lake success as an indication of final victory and roused the Crees under their chiefs Poundmaker and Big Bear to go on the warpath. But in the meantime his support by the white settlers had melted away once blood had been shed, while the Catholic and Protestant missionaries Père Lacombe and John McDougall, had persuaded the uncommitted Indians, including the powerful Blackfoot, to keep the peace. The government in Ottawa moved to meet the legitimate claims of the Métis and a military force of overwhelming strength was being rushed to the West over the new CPR. The odds were too heavy and the battle at Batoche in May, 1885, ended the hopes of the Métis and Indians that the old way of life could be restored. General Middleton's artillery outweighed the expert marksmanship of the Métis. Their cause was lost and Riel's life lost with it. Big Bear and Poundmaker who, like Riel, had given themselves up, were sentenced to two years imprisonment. Louis Riel, tried and condemned for high treason was hanged at Regina in November, 1885. Hero and martyr, traitor and murderer, or guilty but insane — these are three of the estimates of Louis Riel. Who can say, after the years that have passed, which is the right one?

At the first word of the rising of the Métis under Riel and the possibility of an Indian war, Van Horne organized the transport of troops over the still uncompleted railway. He succeeded in moving them from Kingston to Winnipeg in four days as contrasted with Colonel Garnet Wolseley's expedition to the Red River fifteen years earlier which took ninety days. Sir John A. Macdonald found it an easy matter to persuade Parliament to provide additional money for a railway that had so dramatically and effectively shown how useful and necessary it was. On November 7, 1885, in Eagle Pass in the Selkirk range, the line from Ontario to the West was linked with the line started in British Columbia. The Canadian Pacific Railway was complete and East had met West.

George Stephen, (Lord Mount Stephen), who had been the financial genius behind the final drive to complete the railway, named the stop where the link was made, Craigellachie, after the slogan, or war-cry, of Clan Grant with which he had ancestral ties — *Stad Chreag Ealachaidh*, "Stand fast Craigellachie!" Donald Smith, soon to become Lord Strathcona, drove the last, the "golden," spike. On the hundred and fiftieth anniversary (1970) of his birth Canada issued a green, white and gold six-cent stamp showing Smith's head and a stretch of railway track embossed on the head of a golden spike.

. . . . .

Riel's rebellion was scarcely over when the settlers started to flow into the West. Homesteaders flocked westwards from the older provinces of Canada. All through the late 1880s and the 1890s they came, building houses of sod slabs — or in the park areas, of logs — and getting in a crop. It was a hard life and, for many, a struggle just to survive; and above all else it meant hard work, not just for a season but for months and years.

Gradually the type of homesteader changed. The Canadians continued to come but Europeans outnumbered them as the years passed. These were people who saw the Canadian West as a haven of refuge from the poverty, tyranny and oppression of their homelands. They came from Russia and Austria — Doukhobors, Ukrainians, Czechs, Poles, Magyars, Slovaks, Croats — all the races of eastern Europe seeking freedom and land. A considerable number of Mormons, fleeing from persecution in the United States, settled in Alberta in the 1880s and were later joined by many of their co-religionists.

There was a flurry of railway building in the 1890s as younger companies sought to compete with the CPR or to open up areas not served by the older system. Those who had doubted a young and poor country could afford one transcontinental system saw the beginnings of a second take form. This time they had justification for their fears when Canada had about 30,000 miles of track, or one mile of track for every 250 inhabitants. The First World War sent costs upward on a wave of rising prices while freight rates were held down by government order. To prevent complete ruin the Canadian gov-

Three twenty-cent "harvest" stamps — 1929, 1930 and (opposite page) 1946.

ernment was obliged to take over the various independent competitors of the CPR and out of them construct the nationalized system, the Canadian National. But this was not until the end of the war.

During the 1890s and the first decade of the new century, the flow of new settlers became a flood. The American West was pretty well filled up and there was a growing shortage of cheap land. Canada had room to spare and thousands of Americans moved north. The population of Saskatchewan grew from 90,000 to about half a million in ten years while that of Alberta in the same period, 1901-1911, went from 73,000 to 374,000.

As the Territories filled up the settlers pressed for self-government and this came in two steps. In 1888 a Territorial Legislature was set up to replace the autocratic rule under which, since 1875, the lieutenant governor of the Territories had ruled with the assistance of a council of three whom he appointed and whom he could consult if he felt it wise to do so. The new legislature of 1888 had no real powers and though it could debate laws the real power remained with the lieutenant governor just as it had before. When Sir Wilfrid Laurier became prime minister in 1896 his government gave the Territories an executive council appointed by the lieutenant governor, and the chairman of this council became a kind of premier.

Calls for the creation of one or more provinces out of the Territories began to be heard, but Laurier shilly-shallied for several years on the grounds that the population was not large enough and that it would take time to decide how many provinces there should be. The debate went on. Should there be one province or two, or three? If there were two, should one lie to the north of the other, or should they stand side by side? The pressure became so great that something had to be

done, and Laurier, having won the election of 1904, realized the decision could be delayed no longer. In 1905 he brought down a bill to create two provinces, Saskatchewan and Alberta, out of the Northwest Territories and after prolonged and heated debate it was passed in September of that year and the opening of the West was complete.

The set of stamps issued in 1927 to mark the sixtieth anniversary of Confederation includes a twelve-cent dark blue stamp that carries a map of Canada which shows the expansion of the country from its original size in 1867. There were no stamps issued in 1905 to celebrate the entry of two new provinces into the Dominion; but fifty years later, on June 30, 1955, a five-cent ultramarine stamp was issued for the purpose. It carries the names of the two provinces and the dates 1905-1955 and shows a man and a woman in the costume of the last century standing amid wheat and looking toward oil derricks on the horizon, thus indicating the two main supports for the economy of the two provinces. The Royal Canadian Mounted Police had a stamp issued in their honour on June 1, 1935. It is a ten-cent rose-carmine stamp showing a member of the force. The original uniform of the Mounted Police who went into the Territories in the 1870s did not include the familiar broad-brimmed hat. They wore a "pill-box" with a chin-strap and the designers of military millinery never devised anything more inappropriate for the climate of Western Canada. It was replaced by the "Stetson" as shown on the 1935 stamp. The West, once it was settled and supplied with adequate transportation, grew enormous quantities of wheat, and the methods of planting and harvesting changed with the times and the development of technology. Several stamps trace these changes. A twenty-cent dark carmine stamp of 1929 shows wheat being harvested by means of horse-drawn equipment, while a twenty-cent brown-red stamp of 1930 shows more sophisticated machines being drawn by a tractor and, in 1946, a slate-coloured twenty-cent stamp appeared showing an even more advanced combine at work.

Transport & Communication

Perhaps the most difficult problem Canada faced in becoming a nation was one that has not been satisfactorily solved even yet. It is that of distance and communication. Canadians are a thin band of people inhabiting a corridor that reaches from the Atlantic to the Pacific mostly along the 49th parallel of latitude. In order to gain a sense of oneness, of belonging, we should be able to communicate easily with one another in order to understand one another's point of view on matters that must concern us all.

Lord Durham, sent to British North America after the rebellions of 1837 to find some system of government suitable for the North American colonies, is said to have considered briefly the possibility of uniting these colonies into a single country. The idea was quickly dropped as wildly impossible. There was no road between the Maritime Provinces and Lower Canada and no connecting link of any kind between Upper Canada and the distant British trading posts on the Pacific coast. A single nation was clearly out of the question in 1840 if only because of the difficulties of travel and communication.

The Capitulation of Montreal was signed on September 8, 1760, by Vaudreuil, the last French governor, and General Amherst. It surrendered Canada to the British, and the Treaty of Paris three years later merely confirmed the arrangement. Britain never offered, nor did France ask for, the return of the colony. From 1760 onwards for several years Canada was ruled by British military officers. These soldiers left much of the organization of the country undisturbed. The higher French officials had returned to France as quickly as possible after the surrender, but the minor officials, usually Canadian by birth, remained behind and there were soon new notaries and new river pilots, for example, being appointed from among the Canadian population.

Roads, bridges, ferries and posthouses were maintained as before and new roads were begun where they seemed necessary. Travellers between Quebec and Montreal complained

The 1959 St. Lawrence Seaway.

about the highway through Trois-Rivières, and Burton, the British governor there, ordered the road to be widened to thirty feet, with proper ditches. This road became the first land mail route in 1763 when post riders regularly journeyed back and forth from Quebec to Montreal through Trois-Rivières — the three towns, each with a British governor, that were the centres for the military government.

On September 25, 1963, Canada issued a five-cent green and red stamp to commemorate this early postal service. The year before, another stamp had been issued to celebrate the opening of a highway. This was the Trans-Canada Highway which was officially declared open on September 4, 1962, at Rogers Pass, Glacier National Park. It is 4,942 miles in length, one of the longest national highways ever built, and it crosses terrain which had hitherto defeated the efforts of road builders. It made it possible for Canadians to travel from one side of their country to the other without leaving Canadian soil. The road improvements ordered by Lieutenant Colonel Ralph Burton when he was military governor at Trois-Rivières two centuries before had been the beginning of the network of highways that hold a nation within it.

During the early years in Canada after it had passed under British rule travel was as often by water as it was by land. Settlements in Upper and Lower Canada were usually close to a river or a lake and these waterways provided an easy way to travel. The explorers and fur traders had plied them in bark canoes. The bateau and the rather larger Durham boat were used after the War of 1812 both for freight and for passengers. Because there is a fall of nearly six hundred feet on the Great Lakes-St. Lawrence system, on the St. Lawrence Seaway, between Lake Erie and the head of tide at Trois-Rivières, a number of rapids interrupted the flow of traffic. Canals were built around some of these as early as 1779, and at Sault

The 1962 Trans-Canada Highway and the 1963 post rider of 1763.

Ste. Marie the fur-trading North West Company built a canal half a mile long in 1800. A boat canal between Montreal and Lachine and a boat canal at Welland were built within the next twenty-five years and by midcentury ships drawing nine feet of water could sail from salt water to Chicago. By that time, of course, steamships were in use and provided what was for the time the utmost in comfort and speed — a mere two days to cover the distance from Montreal to Toronto.

The long process of taming the rapids and waterfalls in the St. Lawrence River-Great Lakes system was brought into its most advanced stage by the construction of the St. Lawrence Seaway opened officially by Queen Elizabeth II and President Eisenhower of the United States on June 26, 1959. A treaty under which the deep waterway was to be built jointly by Canada and the United States was signed as early as 1932 but nothing was done and the Second World War forced an even longer delay. Canada grew impatient with what seemed to be American reluctance to undertake the project and there were suggestions that the necessary locks and canals might be built entirely on the Canadian side of the St. Lawrence. This did not prove necessary, for the joint undertaking was begun in 1954 and took five years to complete. The new system has a minimum depth of twenty-seven feet and this permits ocean-going ships to sail directly into the Great Lakes and so into the heart of North America.

Canada and the United States each issued a stamp to mark the occasion of the opening of the Seaway. The same design, the Maple Leaf and the American Eagle on a map of the Great Lakes, appears on both stamps. Only the lettering is different.

. . . . .

On land progress was made as well, though more slowly. The road from Quebec to Montreal was well kept and by

Two 1951 stamps commemorating a hundred years of postal service — the four-cent trains and the five-cent steamships.

1800 a posting service equal to those found in Europe served the travelling public. Post houses provided a calèche, a one-horse vehicle capable of carrying two passengers and a driver. It was unsprung, the body hanging from straps, and while not the acme of comfort, perhaps, it was as good as anything available anywhere. In winter the calèche was replaced by a covered sleigh. Speeds of about six miles an hour could be expected. By 1816 stage coaches were running from Montreal to Kingston and within ten years to Toronto, Niagara and Detroit. Many of the better roads in Upper Canada were toll-roads built by private companies, whereas in the Maritime Provinces, perhaps because distances were shorter, a good system of roads, both main and secondary, was built without the use of tolls.

Events taking place in England during this time were to change the methods of travel in Canada and to alter the lives of Canadians. George Stephenson built his first locomotive in 1814 and eleven years later the first public passenger-carrying railway in the world, the Stockton and Darlington Railway, was opened. In 1830 the more famous Liverpool and Manchester Railway was opened. It was built to carry passengers, was double-tracked throughout its thirty-one mile length and covered the distance in an average time of ninety minutes.

The success of these British railways and the beginning of a railway system, sometimes using British locomotives, in the United States moved Canadians to action. The legislature of Lower Canada granted a charter in 1832 to a company to build a railway from Laprairie on the St. Lawrence to St. Johns, sixteen miles away on the Richelieu. By 1852 the railway had grown so that it ran from St. Lambert (Montreal) to Rouses Point, N.Y.

For about ten years this was the only railway operating in British North America, with the exception of a small line

The twenty-cent five stages of mail transport (1927). Opposite page:
The seven-cent stagecoach and airplane (1951).

built in Nova Scotia in 1839 to carry coal from the Albion
mine in Pictou County to loading docks on salt water. The
Albion Mines Railway used a locomotive, the *Sampson*, built
by Timothy Hackworth, a rival and competitor of George
Stephenson. This, the oldest locomotive in North America may
still be seen on display in New Glasgow, N.S.

It was from these small beginnings that Canada's great
railway systems, the world's largest, were developed. First there
were a number of small, struggling lines, such as the St.
Lawrence and Atlantic, the London and Gore Railroad, which
became the Great Western, and the Toronto, Simcoe and
Huron Union Railroad Company, later called the Northern.
The great railway building boom began after 1850. In that
year there were only sixty-six miles of track in British North
America. Ten years later there were over two thousand miles
and the greatest years were yet to come. These saw the building
of the Canadian Pacific to link the Great Plains and British
Columbia to the new Dominion of Canada, and the Inter-
colonial, not to be completed as far as Quebec until 1876 and
to Montreal until 1898, to tie the Maritime Provinces closer
to their partners in Confederation.

In 1951 a series of stamps was issued to commemorate
one hundred years of postal service. Three of these stamps carry
contrasting pictures showing the changes in transport since
1851, the year the three-penny beaver stamp was issued. One
of these stamps, the four-cent dark gray, shows trains of 1851
and 1951. Another, the five-cent purple, similarly demon-
strates steamships and a third, the seven-cent deep blue, shows
a stagecoach and an airplane.

In 1927, on the sixtieth anniversary of Confederation,
a special delivery stamp was brought out. It is a twenty-cent
orange stamp that shows five stages of mail transportation,
from the courier on horseback to the airplane.

If the growth and improvement of transportation systems and methods inside Canada seem remarkable for a country that was young and lacking in population and capital, what was taking place in its traffic with the rest of the world was amazing.

During the middle decades of the last century, a period extending from a short time before Confederation through a short time after it, Canada was the fourth largest ship-owning country in the world. Yarmouth, Nova Scotia, and Saint John, New Brunswick, were among the world's great ship-owning ports, and it is said that the former owned more tons of shipping per head of population than any other port in the world.

Majestic full-rigged ships built in the Maritime Provinces or Quebec carried the products of Canada across the Seven Seas and came home at the end of long voyages with fat profits for their owners — or failed to come home at all. Canadian ships carried hopeful adventurers around the Horn to the California gold fields and a year or two later carried equally hopeful prospectors from British ports to Australia where another "gold rush" was in progress. Soldiers and the materials of war went from England to the Crimea, often enough in ships "built up some Nova Scotian creek" or launched from the shipyards of Saint John or Quebec.

The full story of Canadian shipping in the days of sail is a glorious but neglected part of our history. It began in 1606, when two little vessels were built at Port-Royal, and faded out at the end of the nineteenth century, except for fishing craft, when steel hulls replaced those of wood, when the great pine forests had been cut down and when steam at long last replaced the wind-filled sail as the driving force.

Boats propelled by steam engines had been around a long time. William Symington built the tug *Charlotte Dundas* and sailed her successfully on the Clyde in Scotland five years before the American Robert Fulton steamed up the Hudson River in his *Clermont*. A Canadian-built steam packet, the

The ten-cent brigantine issued by Newfoundland in 1887, and Canada's five-cent Royal William *(1933).*

Accommodation, was running between Quebec and Montreal in 1809 and there was a steam ferry from Quebec to Lévis across the St. Lawrence a few years later.

So far no memorial of the great and prosperous days of the wind-ships has appeared on Canadian stamps. In 1887 Newfoundland issued a ten-cent black stamp depicting a brigantine, while a topsail schooner appears on an even earlier and rarer stamp.

In 1833, however, there occurred an event which is celebrated by the Canadian five-cent blue stamp of 1933 showing a picture of the *Royal William* and commemorating the first transatlantic steamship crossing. Built in 1831 at Cape Cove, Quebec, by John Goudie (a young Scots-Canadian who had learned his trade as a naval architect in Scotland) and fitted with steam engines developing around 200 horsepower, which had been built in Montreal, the *Royal William* was to run between Quebec and Halifax.

She made a few trips, including one to Boston — the first steamship under the British flag to enter a port in the United States. Then her owner decided to send her to England and sell her there. She left Quebec on August 5, 1833, and sailed to Pictou, Nova Scotia, for coal, and cleared for London on August 13. Her clearance papers from Pictou described her: "*Royal William*, 363 tons, 36 men, John McDougall, master. Bound to London. British. Cargo: 253 Chaldrons of coal, a box of stuffed birds and six spars, produce of this Province. One box and one trunk, household furniture and a harp. All British, and seven passengers."

It was probably the last time that Nova Scotia ever exported stuffed birds and a harp to Great Britain, at least in one cargo!

The ship ran into heavy weather, strained her hull and sprang a leak, but Capt. McDougall drove her eastwards with the pumps going and one engine disabled. Twenty-five days after leaving Pictou the *Royal William* docked in London. The first transatlantic passage under steam alone had been accomplished.

She was sold in London and acquired later by the Spanish government which put guns on her and changed her name to *Ysabel Segunda*. Spain was fighting a civil war and she won another distinction. In 1836 she fired the first cannon ever discharged from a steam man-of-war.

. . . . .

Failure to communicate with one another has been given by some historians as a weakness in the fabric of Canadian nationhood. But this is a statement that has a special meaning applied to the lack of clarity and understanding that occurs between people customarily speaking different languages or living in widely differing environments. Judged by the average number of telephone calls made by Canadians (more than by any other people in the world), we communicate freely and, one might suppose, almost continuously.

The man responsible for the means we use to exercise our capacity for talking to one another so frequently was a Scot. He was Alexander Graham Bell who was born in Edinburgh in 1847. His father, and his grandfather, had been interested in the mechanics of speech. Speech studies appealed to him and after formal studies at Edinburgh and London Universities he joined his father in the practice of speech correction and the treatment of speech defects. Two of his brothers died of tuberculosis and, fearing for his own rather delicate health, the family moved to Canada in 1870 and settled near Brantford, Ontario.

It was there while he was working on the transmission and reproduction of sound and the possibility of reproducing sounds visibly for the benefit of the deaf that he hit upon the

The four-cent Alexander Graham Bell, issued in 1947.

idea of the telephone. Here he made the first primitive telephone and here, between Brantford and Paris, Ontario, the first long distance tests were made.

Shortly after his Brantford experiments Bell substituted for his father at a lecture appointment in Boston. He then became a successful teacher of the deaf at Northampton, Massachusetts, and in Boston, where he became the professor of vocal physiology at Boston University. One of his pupils was Mabel Hubbard, the daughter of a wealthy Boston lawyer. She had been deaf since an attack of scarlet fever in childhood. The Hubbards and Alexander Bell formed a warm friendship, and Bell and Mabel were married in 1877. It was a magnificent marriage and his wife's encouragement and influence enriched the life of the young Scot whose main interest was the discovery of ways to improve and benefit the world around him and the people in it.

His interest in the transmission of sound, and therefore of speech, led him after the invention of the telephone, with the fame and wealth that resulted, to experiment with other devices. He invented a phonograph and from its unsatisfactory beginnings he and his associates built the basis for the entire business of modern recording.

In 1885 he and his family visited Nova Scotia and crossed the Bras d'Or Lakes of Cape Breton, stopping for a short time at Baddeck. Bell fell in love with the country which recalled to a homesick Scot the scenes of his native land. The next year he returned to Baddeck, bought property there and began the association that lasted until his death in 1922 — and beyond, for he is buried on the side of Beinn Breagh, the "beautiful mountain," that was for so many years his home.

Bell's restless curiosity and scientific mind led him into researches in a dozen different fields. He carried out valuable studies in heredity. He developed a new breed of sheep. He

The five-cent Silver Dart, *1959 issue.*

invented a surgical probe that was later superseded by X-ray.
He was one of the first, if not the first, to suggest the radium
treatment of cancer and another of his ideas anticipated the
iron lung.

But it was in flight that he made his next contribution.
He worked with a great variety of kites, in an effort to find one
light enough to be supported by air while at the same time
strong enough to support a man and a motor to provide loco-
motion. In 1907 one of his kites, towed by a steamer on Baddeck Bay, carried aloft a passenger and rose 168 feet above
the water.

He gathered about him at Baddeck a group of eager
young engineers among them John A. D. McCurdy and F. W.
(Casey) Baldwin, grandson of the Hon. Robert Baldwin.
Two Americans joined the group, Thomas Selfridge of the
U.S. Army, the passenger of the kite in 1907, who was
destined to die in the crash of one of the Wright brothers'
machines, and Glenn Curtiss, a young manufacturer of motor-
cycles whose name became famous in American aviation. The
group had two headquarters, Beinn Breagh in Canada and
Hammondsport, New York, where Curtiss had his motorcycle
factory. In Hammondsport they built a biplane powered with
a 40-horsepower, V8-cylinder, air-cooled engine designed and
built by Curtiss. Baldwin took it up on March 12, 1908, and
flew it an altitude of ten feet, for 319 feet, and became the
first British subject and the seventh person in the world to fly.

An improved machine was now built and taken to Baddeck. Its engine, once more designed by Curtiss, was more powerful and was water-cooled. Its silken wings were sealed with
rubber to make them airtight. On February 23, 1909, Mc-
Curdy took the new airplane, the *Silver Dart*, up over the ice
of Baddeck Bay and flew half a mile at an altitude of about
thirty feet. A few days later he flew it eight miles in about

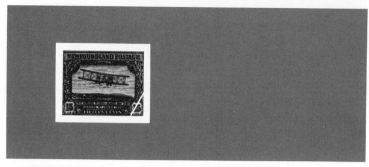

A 1928 Newfoundland stamp celebrating the first non-stop transatlantic flight, by Alcock and Brown in 1919.

eleven minutes. He was the first British subject to fly an airplane in Canada and in the British Empire, though not the first *person* to fly one in the British Empire as is sometimes supposed.

Five more aircraft were built by Bell and his young associates. One of them was taken to Petewawa in 1909 for tests by the Canadian army. Its undercarriage, suitable for landing on ice at Baddeck, folded up when McCurdy landed it on a rough field at Petewawa, and the army in its wisdom decided that aircraft were impractical for military use. Within the next ten years the nation was to thrill with the exploits of the Canadian war aces, Bishop, Barker, Collishaw, Brown, McLeod and a score of others, and in 1919 two British pilots Sir John Alcock and Arthur W. Brown flew one of these impractical contraptions from Newfoundland to Ireland, the first non-stop transatlantic flight.

Canada issued two stamps in honour of Alexander Graham Bell and his contribution to the science of aviation. The first was a four-cent deep blue stamp issued on March 3, 1947, the centenary of Bell's birth. The design of this stamp is so bad that it is embarrassing to think the Canadian Post Office could even have consented to its appearance. It carries a small portrait of Bell against a cloudy background adorned with telegraph or, probably, telephone poles and drooping wires. To one side a winged female figure clad in draperies stands on top of a small globe and extends towards Bell a tiny wreath.

The other Canadian stamp is the five-cent blue-and-black issued on February 23, 1959. It commemorates the flight of the *Silver Dart*, piloted by J. A. D. McCurdy fifty years before. The design shows the little *Silver Dart* airborne against a background of three delta wing jet aircraft. In that one picture the whole story of half a century of aviation is set forth.

A third stamp of more than passing interest is the New-foundland fifteen-cent dark blue issued January 13, 1928, which shows in flight the converted Vickers-Vimy bomber that, in 1919, carried John Alcock and Arthur Brown on the first non-stop transatlantic flight. On the fiftieth anniversary of the flight which began at St. Johns, Newfoundland, and ended in an Irish bog at Clifden 1,890 miles away and sixteen hours and twelve minutes later, Canada issued a stamp commemorating it. This is a fifteen-cent stamp showing the aircraft in flight against a blue-and-green map of the North Atlantic and the lands bordering on it.

The Wars

Modern war has no cheer leaders in Canada. We look on ourselves as a peaceable people with no worldly ambitions likely to lead us into war, and with the very best reasons — we live between two of the world's super-powers — for preventing it from occurring in any part of the world. We send army units halfway around the world to act as keepers of the peace, and give our full support to international peace-keeping organizations as ineffectual now as they are optimistic for the future.

And yet our history is filled with war. Canada has been involved in three wars during the lifetime of many of us, and there are still a few very elderly Canadians who recall a fourth one. As a nation Canada got its start on the Plains of Abraham, saved itself from conquest on Queenston Heights and at Châteauguay and Crysler's Farm, and came of age as a nation on Vimy Ridge. Soldiers "from the wars returning" gave our early settlements the strength to survive; the Carignan-Salières Regiment, the De Meuron, the Watteville, the Royal Highland Emigrants, the Royal Fencible Americans, the King's American Dragoons, DeLancey's Brigade, Butler's Rangers and all those other corps which long ago marched into history now largely forgotten. Our map is studded with military names. Lévis, Wellington, Picton, Brockville, Amherst, Minden, Moncton, Carleton (Sir Guy is also remembered by his title, Dorchester, and rather quaintly, by his first name, Guysboro). Even Lord Rawdon "the Green Dragoon," scourge of the rebels in the South, is not forgotten.

It is a little surprising that with our military past we have not remembered this side of our history more often on our postage stamps. The first stamp with which we did so was the seven-cent olive green stamp carrying the portraits of Wolfe and Montcalm. It was one of the Quebec Tercentenary Issue and appeared on July 16, 1908. On September 10, 1959, a five-cent crimson and dark green stamp was issued for the bicentenary of the battle of the Plains of Abraham.

The Treaty of Aix-la-Chapelle in 1748 officially ended the war between Britain and France but in North America it changed nothing. It did not even bring peace, for warlike activities, like a fire that has been dampened down but not extinguished, sputtered and flared along the disputed boundaries where Americans and Canadians faced one another in the Ohio Valley, in the Lower Great Lakes area and in Acadia. Each side built forts, often on sites indignantly claimed by the opposing side. Each side strove to win the alliance of the Indians or, as a measure of precaution, to defeat and scatter them before they could prove valuable allies to the enemy. Each side went about the business of organizing militia units and training them. Real war, it was clear, was going to be resumed and this time it would be fought to a conclusion.

This time, too, the French in Canada would find the odds heavily against them. The Americans outnumbered them many times to one (1,300,000 to 82,000). New France barely grew enough food to maintain itself and had no surplus left over for the rationing of regular army regiments brought from France, whereas the American colonies had food in abundance. When the Seven Years War did come, Canada had to go on short rations whenever the supply of flour from France was cut off. A high official in France had once suggested that Canadians be encouraged to grow potatoes. His colleagues had pointed out the absurdity of this. Potatoes were too easy to grow. The Canadians would simply grow lazy if they were allowed to cultivate them, and the Indians, if they learned how, would become independant and unmanageable. Besides, potatoes were too bland and tasteless for French palates. The official, ashamed that he had said something silly, dropped the idea.

In 1755 real war erupted in America. Braddock, that haughty Coldstream Guards officer, went to defeat and death in the Ohio Valley. Monckton with his American regiments captured Fort Beauséjour in Acadia.

The next year Canada got a general sent out by France, the Marquis de Montcalm, to take command of all regular army units in New France, and reinforced him with several good regiments of the French army. Louis-Joseph de Montcalm was forty-four years old and had been a soldier since he was fifteen. He had fought in several campaigns in Europe and his promotion up the military ladder had been steady and always for merit, which set him apart from many French officers who depended upon influence at court. Unfortunately for Montcalm, he failed to win the friendship of Vaudreuil, the governor. The Marquis de Vaudreuil was the first native-born Canadian to be governor of Canada (he was to be the last of his race to hold that office for two hundred years) and like the majority of Canadians of that time he resented the French, finding them arrogant and superior and inclined to patronize the Canadians. The two men on whom the survival of Canada depended pulled in opposite directions at a time when their close collaboration was essential.

Montcalm had to carry out his task of defending Canada under the critical eye of the unfriendly governor; to get his supplies from the intendant, Bigot, who was a corrupt grafter intent on bleeding the government of France, the Indians, the army and the people; and to depend for support on a mother country, France, that was bored with Canada and could not afford the drain on its finances which Canada always seemed to require. Madame de Pompadour ruled France, and under her direction France kept its eyes on Europe, all its military strength directed to the help of its new ally, Austria. There was little to spare for Canada, which one of Madame's literary friends described as "a country inhabited by bears, beavers and barbarians, and covered eight months of the year with snow." The French had never really cared for Canada, so if poor Montcalm had to lose it no one would very much mind. Good riddance!

The British attitude to the war was exactly opposite that

of France. William Pitt the Elder came to office in 1756. He was not a member of the tired old nobility but the grandson of a man who had gone to India and there acquired a great fortune. Pitt believed in colonies. Britain was a commercial nation and colonies gave her markets and raw materials. His policy was to leave the land fighting in Europe mostly in the very capable hands of Britain's ally Frederick the Great of Prussia, while the Royal Navy and whatever troops could be mustered were given to bright, ambitious, thrusting young officers and used to relieve France of her overseas possessions. So he sent Clive to India, Jeffrey Amherst, Lord Howe and James Wolfe to America.

Not all his plans succeeded. Howe was killed in a minor skirmish; and the British commander-in-chief Abercrombie, for whom Howe was to supply the drive and perhaps the brains, was badly beaten at Ticonderoga (1758) by Montcalm with his French regulars, Canadians and a swarm of Indians. Like Braddock before him, Abercrombie had artillery but omitted to use it, although any American serving with him could have told him that the certain way to clear a battlefield of Indians, and possibly of Canadian militia, was to send grapeshot whistling about their ears.

Ticonderoga was offset by Amherst's capture of Louisbourg. James Wolfe, one of Pitt's young men, led his Grenadiers ashore through the booming surf of Gabarus Bay and established a bridgehead from which the British regiments broke out to encircle the town and its fort. Wolfe was the leader who directed the attack and the best the Louisbourg garrison could do was to prolong the siege until it was too late for the British to besiege Quebec before winter closed the St. Lawrence to their supporting ships. A good deal of the credit for that meagre success was probably due to the wife of Louisbourg's governor. Madame de Drucourt, "La Bombardière," proved to be the boldest soldier of them all, never letting a day pass without firing three cannon shots at the

The seven-cent Montcalm and Wolfe, issued in 1908.

British in defiance, and to encourage the garrison.

1759 was the year of victory, "the wonderful year," with victories in Europe at Minden and Quiberon Bay. In America the French lost Niagara, and Amherst, advancing up the old invasion route to Canada, defeated them at Ticonderoga. The main British attack, however, was at Canada's capital, Quebec. In the eighteenth century to lose the capital to the enemy was to suffer the heaviest blow of all, probably to lose the war itself.

Wolfe, now a major general at the age of thirty-two, arrived before Quebec with three brigades of infantry, auxiliary companies of Rangers and units of artillery. The whole force was carried on transports guarded by forty-five ships of the Royal Navy, and altogether there were 170 ships manned by eighteen thousand seamen. One of the pilots who brought this armada up the river was that Captain James Cook, the great explorer whose picture appears on the stamps of Australia, New Zealand and the Cook Islands but not on the stamps of Canada.

Montcalm had had ample warning of the attack from captured despatches describing the British plans. He had more troops, of a kind, than Wolfe and he placed these between the St. Charles River behind Quebec and the Montmorency where it flowed into the St. Lawrence. Here, with his army in trenches and behind earthworks, he hoped to keep Wolfe from landing on the north shore of the St. Lawrence and avoid battle until the approach of autumn storms and the threat of winter should cause the fleet to withdraw, taking Wolfe and his army with it. Quebec, perched on its rocky headland, was believed to be impregnable but he gave it a garrison of more than a thousand men under the command of the Canadian, De Ramezay.

It was a good plan but ignored the boldness of the Brit-

The five-cent stamp issued in 1959 to mark the bicentenary of the battle of the Plains of Abraham.

ish navy because it assumed that the ships would not pass the narrows before Quebec and go upstream to threaten the supply route to the city. Admiral Saunders sent H.M.S. *Sutherland* with four small armed vessels above the city. Later a flotilla of flat-bottomed boats passed upstream, raiding parties went ashore and Montcalm was obliged to weaken his army below Quebec in order to strengthen it west of the capital. In the meantime Monckton's guns were slowly destroying the city by shellfire from across the St. Lawrence.

The next British move was to try to get ashore at the Montmorency but fire from the ships could not silence the French batteries and the timing of the attack went wrong when the Grenadiers landed too soon. The British were repulsed with heavy losses that would have been even larger had not a heavy rainstorm wet the powder and put an end to the fighting.

The weeks went by and no way could be found to bring Montcalm to battle. Wolfe, never in good health, fell ill and slowly recovered. He suggested another attack on the Montmorency lines but his brigadiers made the counter-suggestion that a landing be attempted above Quebec and to this Wolfe agreed. He changed the plan of the brigadiers, however, by going in person to find a landing place closer to the city than they had suggested. There was a French force upstream under the command of Bougainville (who was later to give his name to the well-known flowering vine), and Wolfe had no intention of putting his landing party ashore where it would have to fight back-to-back against two attacking French armies. He found the place he wanted in the Anse-du-Foulon (Wolfe's Cove), just as he had found the right undefended spot on Gabarus Bay the year before.

On the night of September 12 the landing force was assembled in thirty flat-bottomed boats. Wolfe himself was with a small group of twenty-four picked men. The boats set out on the ebb tide, and as it gathered speed they drifted rapidly down the river. The leading boats were carried beyond the landing place but Wolfe leaped ashore and with his picked men scrambled up the cliff and gained the top unnoticed. There they overpowered the sleepy guard, and the little British force immediately began to climb up the path from the Anse-du-Foulon. By six o'clock in the morning Wolfe was lining up his army in two ranks, just under five thousand men, the best soldiers, eighteenth century style, who had ever set foot on American soil.

Four hours later Montcalm's army hurried out of its defensive positions and moved forward to attack the British line. The Canadian militia sat on the ground to reload after each shot (as a hundred years later the Confederate soldiers did in the American Civil War), so that the French advance was ragged and irregular. Wolfe's orders to his superb troops was to hold their fire until the enemy was within twenty-five yards — the width of a city street. The French and Canadians advanced in three columns and were met as they neared the British line with what one writer described as "the most perfect volley ever fired on battlefield," a thunderclap, a deafening crash, as if from a single monstrous weapon. The British line then stepped forward and fired again, a step and a volley, for from six to eight minutes. As the smoke cleared the French were seen to be retreating in confusion. The battle had lasted hardly a quarter of an hour. Wolfe was dead and Montcalm was dying, crying as he was steadied in his saddle, "It is nothing! Do not distress yourselves for me, my friends!"

Monckton, next senior to Wolfe, was wounded and the command passed to George Townshend who had been jealous of Wolfe and probably had intrigued against him. His brother Charles, was a member of Pitt's cabinet, though he was later to desert Pitt for another leader when it seemed likely to advance his interests. He was also the man who put the tax on tea which so infuriated the Americans and was one of the steps leading to the American Revolution. Perhaps the Townshend propaganda has had it effect on those recent crtitics who, looking back with the wisdom that two hundred years' hindsight confers, have discounted Wolfe's ability as a military leader. The Townshends worked hard to injure him. The political Townshend once said publicly, "Of course my brother writes all Wolfe's despatches." The celebrated wit George Selwyn was present and with the slight stammer that gave point to his remarks, said. "D-does he, indeed! Then wh-who writes your b-brother's?"

When quiet descended once more that September day on the fields once tilled by Abraham Martin, one régime had ended and another had begun. Wolfe and Montcalm who appear, side by side, on the seven-cent olive green stamp issued a century and a half later probably never saw one another in life. They undoubtedly respected one another's ability and they shared one defect in judgment. As experienced professionals, men from the mother countries, they tended to undervalue the local militia, to look down on colonials. Perhaps that was why Vaudreuil and De Ramezay gave Montcalm less help than he asked for and needed on the day of battle. It was an attitude that Wolfe's successors maintained twenty years years later during the American Revolution, even the admired Guy Carleton sometimes failing to hide his belief that the colonials were a lesser breed. It probably, if any one cause could be blamed, cost Britain the loss of the Thirteen Colonies.

. . . . .

Canada had little part in the American Revolutionary War. An American army under Benedict Arnold and Richard Montgomery attacked Quebec on New Year's Eve, 1775, after a remarkable winter march that was itself a great

military exploit. Montgomery, an Irish ex-officer of the British army, was killed almost at the first moment of the attack and Arnold, who had been badly wounded, retired to Montreal and eventually back home. The only other fighting was a brief affair in Nova Scotia when some local rebels organized an "army" and tried to capture Fort Cumberland. While they were trying to think of some method of overcoming the fort's resistance two companies of the Royal Emigrants Regiment arrived on the scene and put Jonathan Eddy and his army into full flight with a single volley of musketry.

The war with Napoleon was a different matter. It lasted, with two short interludes of peace, from 1793 to 1815, and for considerable portions of that time Britain was fighting for her existence.

Napoleon, in 1806, attacked Britain by the application of economic warfare. He issued the First Berlin Decree which declared "the British Isles are in a state of blockade," and all commerce with them was forbidden as was trade with British colonies. Additional decrees strengthened and extended the first one. He was unable to enforce the blockade beyond the coastlines of Europe because the Royal Navy had control of the seas. Even then there were loopholes through which British goods slipped into European markets. Napoleon had to shut his own eyes on certain occasions, such as when his quartermasters by roundabout methods obtained good British boots and thick woolen cloth from Yorkshire with which to make greatcoats for a French army shivering in the bitter depths of a Polish winter.

But the decrees were successful in another direction. They involved Britain in a dispute with the United States. Britain had replied to the decrees by declaring a blockade against France and this gave the Americans grounds for complaint. The British navy claimed "the right of search," too, and began stopping American vessels on the high seas to search for deserters from the British service. They even stopped

The Guernsey four-penny Brock issued in 1969. Opposite page: The 1969 Canada six-cent Brock with the monument at Queenston Heights.

the U.S.S. *Chesapeake* and took off some deserters but killed an American in the process. The Americans were outraged and Britain apologized.

How much British interference with American trade and the exercise of the right of search contributed to the outbreak of war is a matter of opinion. New England, where a great part of the shipping of the United States was owned, opposed the war and through a system of licences obtained from British authorities traded happily with the Maritime Provinces and the West Indies throughout the conflict.

The real demand for war with the British came from the noisy "war hawk" party led by the windy orator Henry Clay of Kentucky. The "war hawks" were moved by hatred of Britain, greed to exploit the lands belonging to the Indian tribes of the West and the belief that Canada could be had, as former President Thomas Jefferson said, "through a mere matter of marching." Urged on by Clay, Andrew Jackson and the other warmongers, the United States declared war on Great Britain. Boston merchants flew flags at half-mast to show their disapproval of "Mr. Madison's war."

Canadians were aghast at the prospect of war in which the enemy outnumbered them so heavily. When the war began there were fewer than thirty thousand soldiers in Canada, less than a third of them trained regulars. The United States could put thirty-five thousand regulars in the field and militia numbering three or four times that number. Fortunately for Canada the American militia, though often individually courageous and expert riflemen, proved to be just about the worst soldiers in the world. The regular army was not much better, and they were commanded by a set of blundering and inept generals. Even more fortunately, Canada had as acting lieutenant governor of Upper Canada and commander of the army, Colonel Isaac Brock.

The Guernsey five-penny and 1/9 Brock stamps of 1969. Opposite page:
The Guernsey 2/6 Brock of 1969.

Brock, a native of Guernsey, stood six foot two and every inch was soldier. When the Shawnee chief Tecumseh met him and discussed the situation he turned to his warriors and the other Indian leaders and said, "This is a *man!*" Brock was forty-three and had been an army officer for twenty-eight of those years, attaining the rank of colonel after only thirteen years.

Had the Americans advanced on Montreal and cut Upper and Lower Canada apart the war might have ended quickly; but they chose instead to attack in the West, and the comic opera general to whom command was given was William Hull. Hull crossed the Detroit River, occupied the village of Sandwich and sat down to wonder what to do next. While he wondered word reached him that the British had captured Fort Michilimackinac at the entrance to Lake Michigan and that the Indians, encouraged by this British success, were beginning to ally themselves with the Canadians. This news, together with notice that Brock was approaching, caused Hull to re-cross the Detroit River. Brock with a little force of seven hundred men, most of them drawn from the 41st Foot but including one unit fighting far from home, the Royal Newfoundland Fencibles, pursued Hull across the river and demanded his surrender. Hull refused at first though he was terrified by the war-whoops of the Indians. One shell from Brock's artillery burst in the officers' mess in Fort Detroit and changed Hull's mind immediately. He surrendered at once and was soon on his way to sit out the war as a prisoner in Quebec.

Shortly afterward the Americans made a thrust into Canada across the Niagara River. On the morning of October 13, 1812, American regular army units and their deplorable militia began to cross the river to attack Queenston Heights. Brock was at Fort George and immediately took horse to ride

to Queenston. He found the Americans swarming ashore. Sending a messenger back to order up the garrison of Fort George, he put himself at the head of a little group of about a hundred men and led a charge to dislodge the Americans from the Heights. The Americans gave way, but one, stepping from the bush, shot Brock at point blank range, killing him almost instantly. Lt. Col. John Macdonell launched a second attack and was killed in his turn. But by this time General Roger Sheaffe, a Loyalist born in Boston, arrived with reinforcements, including a unit composed of Negroes and, fixing bayonets, drove the Americans back towards the river.

    The officer who had taken charge of the Americans was Lt. Col. Winfield Scott who played a prominent part later in the war with Mexico and was the commanding general of the United States Army in Washington in 1861 when the Civil War broke out. On this occasion, his army reduced to a huddled mass penned against the Niagara River, he fluttered a white handkerchief in surrender and greatly embarrassed Sheaffe who found himself with more prisoners than he had soldiers.

    Brock's victory at Detroit and the battle of Queenston Heights set the tone for the entire war. There were reverses at Chippewa and Moraviantown. The Americans burned York (Toronto). But De Salaberry's victory over Wade Hampton at Châteauguay and Morrison's defeat of Wilkinson at Crysler's Farm in 1813 put a satisfactory conclusion to war in which English and French Canadians had stood shoulder to shoulder in defence of their country.

    In 1969 Canada issued a six-cent stamp showing Brock's portrait and the towering monument erected in his honour on the battlefield of Queenston Heights. The stamp commemorates the bicentenary of his birth. His native island of Guernsey also issued four stamps in his honour in 1969. One is a four-penny stamp bearing his portrait, the head of Queen Elizabeth as is required on all British stamps, and a

Canadian maple leaf. Two of the others are also portraits while the fourth shows the arms of Canada of 1812 and several flags including the present Canadian one.

. . . . .

After the Treaty of Ghent ended the war Canada was not involved in any large war for a very long time. There were some domestic disturbances, the rebellions of 1837, 1870 and 1885 that called for the use of troops, but they were in reality pretty small affairs. British North Americans engaged, as individuals, in British wars abroad. In the Crimean War, Colonel Dunn won the first Victoria Cross given a Canadian and Fenwick Williams, a Nova Scotian, was given a baronetcy for his long defence of Kars against the Russian army invading Asiatic Turkey. In the Indian mutiny Sir John Inglis took command of besieged Lucknow and William Hall, a fellow Nova Scotian, won a Victoria Cross with the column sent to relieve him. Inglis was the son of the Bishop of Nova Scotia and Hall the son of black slaves rescued from their American owner during the War of 1812. History does not record that the two ever met. None of these has appeared on Canadian stamps, nor has Canadian participation in the South African War, 1899-1902, been commemorated postally.

The two Great Wars of the twentieth century cost Canada heavily in lives and treasure. Volumes have been written to explain why the First World War (1914-1918) began, but Canada and Canadians had had no share in the construction of the elaborate system of alliances and counter-alliances, the imperial ambitions and expansionist policies of the European powers. It was a world of diplomatic arrangements, espionage, plots and counterplots and when a Serbian student assassinated an Austrian archduke few Canadians knew or cared. The shots that Gavrilo Princip fired that June day

The one-cent Newfoundland Suvla Bay issued in 1919.

in the street of a Bosnian town applied a spark to the long fuse the statesmen of Europe had laid to a powder barrel. Once lit no one was able to stop it and the powder barrel exploded. The powder barrel was Europe itself.

The position of Canada within the British Empire in 1914 made it automatic for her to be at war when Great Britain was. Canada did have the right to decide which part she would play in such a war and in 1914 the decision was to give every possible support to Great Britain and her allies. Canadians served in the navy, the army and in the air force that developed into an important weapon during the war. The first Canadians to lose their lives through enemy action were midshipmen lost when German battle cruisers sank H.M.S. *Monmouth* and H.M.S. *Good Hope* off Coronel, Chile, in October 1914.

An appeal for volunteers for the army was answered by a rush of men to enlist and an expeditionary army numbering over thirty-two thousand men sailed for England at the end of September 1914. Twenty-eight North Atlantic passenger liners packed with soldiers protected by four light cruisers of the Royal Navy set out for Britain and were joined during the crossing by two more ships carrying the Newfoundland Contingent. A long period of training was needed to turn the volunteer army into an efficient fighting force. It was February 1915 before the 1st Canadian Division landed in France and in April it was marched north to form part of the defensive line at Ypres in Belgium.

Newfoundland was not to become a part of Canada for thirty-four years and the Newfoundland Regiment, which built up a reputation for great courage and suffered enormous casualties in the war, did not form part of the Canadian army. It was attached to a British division (the 29th) and sent out to the Dardanelles. Put into the trenches at Suvla Bay it

The fifteen-cent Alcock and Brown memorial issued by Canada in 1969.

hung on grimly under heavy fire from Turkish artillery until the whole idea of forcing the Dardanelles was given up and the army there withdrawn and returned to England.

The first battle for the Canadians began on April 22, 1915. It was here at Gravenstafel Ridge and St. Julien that the German army made the first successful use of poison gas as a weapon. Five thousand cylinders of chlorine gas was released to be carried into the lines of the Allied armies defending Ypres.

So strange and horrible was the mysterious green cloud that swirled into their trenches and filled their throats and lungs with agony that the French gave way to panic and fled, leaving a wide gap between the Canadian division and the British Second Army. The next four days saw the Canadians engaged in a desperate battle against some of the best divisions of professional soldiers in the German army. Much of the fighting was against an enemy still launching chlorine for which there was no defence except an ineffective wet cloth across the mouth and nose. They held their ground against attack and rocked the enemy back by furious and unexpected counter-attacks. When it was over and the German thrust had been parried, the British War Office made the statement that the Canadians "undoubtedly saved the situation."

Its fame as a fighting force gained at Ypres in 1915 continued and grew as the war dragged its seemingly endless way into the next year and the next. New divisions came to join the First and the Canadian Corps was formed and commanded by a Canadian general, Sir Arthur Currie. The list of battles fought by Canadian troops grew and the fields of white crosses grew as well: the Somme, Amiens, Courcelette, Arras, Beaumont Hamel, Messines, Cambrai, Canal-du-Nord, Ypres again and all the others — and Vimy Ridge.

Vimy was the turning point of the war in France.

The fifteen-cent Vimy Memorial stamp issued in 1968.

The Ridge is not very high, less than five hundred feet, but it stands in flat country which makes it an important feature from a soldier's point of view. It is not very long, either, only about four miles. It slopes in a gradual ascent from west to east and drops off steeply once the crest is reached. Marlborough's army fought a small battle there during the War of the Spanish Succession.

In the Spring of 1917 it was in German hands. The Germans had no intention of giving it up and had already defended it successfully against attacks by the French. They had fortified it with trenches, tunnels, deep shelters and concrete strongpoints. Some distance behind it lay the French industrial city of Lille and its surrounding mines. Vimy had to be retained.

This was the object the Canadians had to attack on the morning of April 9, Easter Monday, 1917. All the preparations had been made, the troops specially trained, every movement rehearsed over and over again. The massed guns of the artillery were ready. Huge dumps of shells had been assembled, being brought upon specially built railroads and roads built of planks. Arrangements were ready for the rescue and removal of the wounded. Everything to do with a battle, it was hoped, had been foreseen and attended to.

The guns opened fire on April 2 and poured thousands of shells on the German positions steadily for a week, right up to zero hour which was at 5:30 A.M. At precisely that moment, in a cold sleet storm, the Canadians in three waves, advanced on the German lines. By 8 A.M. the First and Third Divisions had reached the crest of the ridge. The Fourth Division which formed the left wing of the advance faced greater resistance but that, too, was overcome. The Canadian Corps stood proud and self-confident, its men fit and trained, sure that no army on either side was its superior in the arts

The two-cent National War Memorial, Ottawa, issued in 1939.

of war and fully aware that it was the army of a new nation, strong, independent and free.

Vimy was to be the first of a long roll call of victories spread over the next year and a half. There were forty thousand Canadian troops — labour battalions, railway troops, tunnellers and other special units — that were not in the Canadian Corps. And there were thousands of Canadians in the Royal Flying Corps and its successor, the Royal Air Force, where they performed brilliantly as fighter pilots. The Corps itself in the "last hundred days" of the war extended its record of unbroken victory by advancing 86 miles, defeating 47 German divisions and capturing 31,500 prisoners and 623 cannon. On the morning of November 11, 1918, the day the war ended, the Canadian army marched into Mons, from which the British army had been forced by the massive German advance more than four years before.

In 1938 Canada issued a ten-cent stamp showing the Memorial Chamber of the Peace Tower. In this Chamber the following inscription referring to the men fallen in the wars may be read.

They are too near
To be great
But our children
Shall understand
Where and how
Our fate was changed
And by whose hand.

In 1939 King George VI and Queen Elizabeth visited Ottawa and while there unveiled the magnificent National War Memorial designed by the brothers Vernon and Sydney March. Sculptured figures in bronze, representing

*The ten-cent Memorial Chamber in the Peace Tower, Ottawa, issued in
1938.*

Canadians at war, pass through an arch. The Navy, the
Army, the Air Force, the Medical Corps press forward in
lifelike reality. A two-cent black and brown stamp depicting
this monument was issued that same year.

A Canadian War Memorial was unveiled at Vimy
Ridge on July 26, 1936, by King Edward VIII to celebrate
the event: "So high it soars it can be seen a countryside
away . . . Around its ramparts, below the vast twin pylons
which stand for the armies of Canada and of France, are
engraved the names of nigh twelve thousand men of the
Dominion who have no known resting place."[1]

France issued two postage stamps on that date, a
seventy-five-centime henna brown and a one-and-a-half-franc
dull blue stamp. Each carries a picture of the great white
memorial whose designer and sculptor was Walter Allward.
Canada, of course, has also, in 1968, issued a stamp showing
the Vimy Memorial, or a least an important part of it. This
stamp a fifteen-cent slate-black shows "The Defenders" and
"The Breaking of the Sword," two of the sculptures forming
part of the Memorial.

Newfoundland in 1919 issued a set of stamps "The
Trail of the Caribou Issue" in which each stamp bears the
name of a battle in which the Newfoundland Regiment fought,
for example, Suvla Bay, Monchy, Beaumont Hamel, or it
carries the inscription "Royal Naval Reserve" and the Latin
motto *Ubique* — "Everywhere."

. . . . .

When the First World War ended, and the Treaty of Versailles in 1919 not only brought peace but established a League

---

[1] James Spence, in *Canadian Geographical Journal*, July 1936.

Two 1942 stamps: the twenty-cent corvette and the thirteen-cent "Ram" tank.

of Nations whose principal task was to preserve that peace forever, it seemed for a short time that perhaps the war just concluded really had been "the war to end all wars." Twenty years later the League of Nations was in ruins, the world's hopes for peace had vanished in the smoke rising from burning Polish cities and the Second World War, 1939-1945, had ended the fragile peace established by the Treaty of Versailles.

Once more Canada fought for democracy and to defeat dictatorship, and once more the cost in lives and treasure was high. Fought for much the same reasons as the First World War and with more or less the same line-up on each side, the two wars were very different in the way they were conducted. The great difference between them was the result of the rapid development of technology, much of it stimulated by the First World War, which equipped the opposing sides with weapons far in advance of anything ever seen on battlefields before. In 1914 men had gone to war in airplanes that were scarcely more than flimsy kites made of wood and fabric and powered with small and not very efficient engines. By 1939 the airplane was a very fast, heavily armed weapon whose skilful use was quite capable of deciding battles on land or sea and changing the whole course of war.

The first tank battle was at Cambrai in 1917. Only 378 fighting tanks were used in that battle. They were successful in their day even if they were clumsy to handle, had many mechanical problems and could only communicate with one another successfully by the use of semaphore. By 1940 the skilful use of large groups of tanks, combined with equally skilful use of aircraft, defeated Poland in a matter of days and knocked France out of the war in weeks.

Where the First World War was one of fixed lines of fortifications — the long trench system that reduced army

The fifty-cent munitions factory and the one-dollar destroyer, both issued in 1942.

movements to a matter of a few yards, a mile or two at a time — the Second World War was one of speed and rapid movement.

Once again Canadians fought on land, at sea and in the air. Once again Canadian factories produced the weapons and materials of war. But in the interval between the two wars Canada had become an industrialized nation capable of manufacturing the complicated and very technical weapons of the day.

The set of stamps issued by Canada carry in pictures a little of the story of the country's part in the war. Three of the stamps show the portrait of King George VI in the uniforms of the three services — Navy, Army and Air Force. The thirteen-cent (in 1943 changed to fourteen-cent) dull green stamp shows a "Ram" tank; the twenty-cent chocolate brown, a corvette under construction in a shipyard. In this war the Royal Canadian Navy carried a very much heavier and more important share of the country's war effort than it had in the earlier war, particularly in the protection of convoys carrying essential supplies across the Atlantic. The corvette and, a little later, the slightly larger and more powerful frigate were the types of ships built in Canada and much used in this convoy work. They supplemented the work done by the much bigger, faster and more heavily armed destroyers such as that shown on the one-dollar deep blue stamp issued in this series. The fifty-cent violet stamp shows a scene in a munitions plant where men are at work assembling 25-pounder field guns.

In the United States and in France it is not unusual for postage stamps to appear carrying the portrait of outstanding military figures. In countries of the British Commonwealth the practice is little followed although Canada has gone farther than the others with stamps commemorating four generals.

Perhaps other fighting men — Dorchester, Williams, Currie, Simcoe, Lévis, Le Moyne de Longueuil and others — will be honoured. There are a number of women whose military exploits might well be remembered. Madame La Tour, Madame de Drucourt — perhaps, if historians can reach agreement on her, even Laura Secord.

Arts & Letters

Several countries have issued stamps in memory of their great poets, playwrights or prose writers. Great Britain, in 1964, printed five stamps celebrating the four-hundredth anniversary of the birth of Shakespeare. These interesting stamps, each of which illustrates some moment in one of his most famous plays, was followed the next year by two stamps carrying the portrait of Robert Burns, Scotland's favourite poet. France has produced stamps in honour of many of her famous sons, including Corneille, La Fontaine, Mistral, Stendhal and Fénelon. The United States, too, has recognized literary men as suitable subjects for commemoration on stamps. Thoreau, Francis Parkman, England's Shakespeare and Italy's Dante have all appeared on American stamps.

. . . . .

In 1961 Canada produced a stamp bearing the portrait of Emily Pauline Johnson (1862-1913), the Mohawk poetess born on the Six Nations Indian Reserve at Brantford, Ontario. Her poetry, collected in a book entitled *Flint and Feather*, was very popular at the beginning of the century and thousands of people went to hear her recite her poems when she made long tours across Canada speaking in theatres, church halls and schoolhouses. In "The Corn Husker" she describes a woman of her race come to glean corn missed by the harvesters:

> *Age in her fingers, hunger in her face*
> *Her figure stooped with weight of work and years,*
> *But rich in tawney colouring of her race*
> *She comes a-field to strip the purple ears.*

. . . . .

Another poet, Dr. John McCrae (1872-1918), appears on the stamp issued October 15, 1968, the fiftieth anniversary of his death of influenza in the great epidemic that swept across the war-weary world in late 1918. McCrae, who was born in

The six-cent Stephen Leacock (1969) and the five-cent John McCrae (1968).

Guelph, Ontario, served with great distinction in the Medical Corps in the First World War and wrote the very famous "In Flanders Fields," which is probably the best-known poem ever written by a Canadian. The stamp carries McCrae's portrait and a picture of a First World War battlefield dotted with ". . . the crosses, row on row,/That mark our place . . ." Over the battlefield with its soldiers' graves appear the title and first lines of his poem.

. . . . .

The third Canadian writer to appear on a postage stamp was Stephen Leacock (1869-1944), and the Canadian postal authorities printed thirty-four million of them. Canada has produced a number of humorists of international renown, beginning with the Nova Scotian Thomas Chandler Haliburton (1796-1865), whose book *The Clockmaker; or, The Sayings and Doings of Sam Slick of Slickville* has been called the first great humorous writing in North America. Haliburton, though he has an area in Ontario named after him, has yet to be honoured by a stamp.

Leacock, who was born in England and brought to Canada when he was still a small boy, became a teacher when he grew up. He taught for eight years at Upper Canada College and, having continued his own education, he later became professor of political economy at McGill University. All the while he was writing witty and comic sketches and essays or short stories filled with pure fun. Some of them aimed at the exposure of pomposity and sham, or revealed the silly aspects of things most people accepted without question. But there was never any malice in Leacock's nonsense and he laughed with people rather than at them. He is, with the possible exception of Lucy Maud Montgomery, creator of the

The eight-cent "Alaska Highway" by A. Y. Jackson and the ten-cent "Jack Pine" by Tom Thomson, both issued in 1967.

immortal *Anne of Green Gables*, probably the best-known and most widely read Canadian author. His work has been translated into other languages, including Russian.

Just what Leacock would have thought of the idea of his appearance on a stamp is difficult to judge. Every man is pleased to be honoured by his country. But Leacock in one of his books poked some gentle fun at his fellow professors of political economy and their solemn theories about the origins of countries and governments.

He said that when some area contained enough people who felt they needed stamps they got together and set up a government so that it could issue some. "If the stamps are to have a man's head as the design, the country is placed under a king, the king having the kind of features needed for a stamp." There were drawbacks, of course — "The Emperor of Brazil had to be deposed in 1889, his whiskers being too large to go through the Post. . . ."

. . . . .

In recent years a number of countries have issued stamps bearing reproductions of art masterpieces produced by their citizens. In 1967 Canada, too, offered stamps carrying reproductions of the work of its artists. Seven stamps display paintings of Canadian scenes. Unfortunately each stamp is printed in a single colour although multicoloured reproductions of paintings no longer present much of a printing problem and very beautiful multicoloured art stamps had been issued, for example, by New Zealand (paintings by Rembrandt, Sassoferrato, Murillo and Titian), Belgium and Great Britain, to name only three countries.

Though the Canadian postal authorities missed an opportunity to give us a series of spectacularly beautiful

The fifteen-cent "Bylot Island" of Lawren Harris and the twenty-five-cent "The Solemn Land" of J. E. H. MacDonald, both issued in 1967.

stamps they did, at least, recognize that art plays a part in Canadian life. The series consists of an eight-cent violet brown reproduction of A. Y. Jackson's "Alaska Highway," a ten-cent olive green copy of Tom Thomson's celebrated "The Jack Pine," a fifteen-cent dull purple view of Lawren Harris's "Bylot Island," and a twenty-five cent slate green copy of J. E. H. MacDonald's "The Solemn Land." Three of these artists were members of the famous Group of Seven with which the name of Tom Thomson is usually associated although he was never a member and indeed was dead before it was formed.

Of the remaining three stamps "The Quebec Ferry," a twenty-cent dark blue stamp is from the painting by James Wilson Morrice (1865-1924); "Summer's Stores," a painting of grain elevators near Sexsmith, Alberta, by Arthur John Ensor is on a fifty-cent brownish orange stamp; and "Imperial Wildcat No. 2 Excelsior Field, Alberta" by Henry George Glyde completes the set with a one-dollar crimson rose stamp.

Arthur John Ensor and Henry George Glyde are natives of Great Britain though both have lived in Canada for more than thirty years. James Wilson Morrice won fame in Europe as an artist and in France he was often referred to as "The Painter of Paris." His paintings hang in the Louvre in Paris, in the Tate Gallery in London and in the National Gallery, Washington. Much of his career was in Europe and North Africa and he died in Tunis in 1924.

In 1969 Canada issued its first multicoloured art stamp. This is the fifty-cent stamp issued March 14, 1969, which reproduces "Return from the Harvest Field," painted by Aurèle de Foy Suzor-Côté (1869-1937). It celebrates the centennial of the birth of this artist, a native of Arthabaska, Quebec, who studied and painted in France for some years

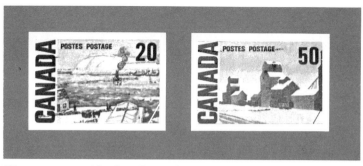

The twenty-cent "Quebec Ferry" by J. W. Morrice and the fifty-cent "Summer's Stores" by A. J. Ensor. Overleaf: The one-dollar "Imperial Wildcat No. 2" by H. G. Glyde. All issued in 1967.

before returning to Canada. His work was of such distinction that he was honoured by the French Academy in 1901. Equally at home as a figure or landscape artist, Suzor-Côté interpreted the life of rural Quebec and he did so with sincerity and great technical skill.

. . . . .

Tom Thomson (1877-1917) is probably the best-known name among Canadian artists. His sudden death and the mystery that many believed to surround it have made him known even to those who are unfamiliar with his paintings. He was born at Claremont, Ontario, went to school in Owen Sound and, after working a short time as a commercial artist in the United States, he went to Toronto and got a job with a firm that made engravings. It employed a good many artists some of whom took up landscape painting as a change from their commercial work, and for recreation. Thomson was associated with these men though he did not begin outdoor sketching at the same time as the others. But once he begån to paint landscapes he rapidly became a brilliant painter who thoroughly understood the Canadian north country and caught its peculiar beauty in an amazing group of canvases all done within the short time of five years. His death by drowning in Canoe Lake deprived Canada of a native-born genius while his work was only at its beginning.

J. E. H. MacDonald had worked at the same engraving shop as Thomson. He was born in England of Canadian parents, and his family returned to Canada when he was thirteen. He was persuaded by Lawren Harris, another of the artists represented in this set of stamps, to give up commercial work and devote himself to painting. Success did not

come to him as quickly as it had to Thomson, but his sense of design, the originality of his use of colour and the feeling of immensity he was able to give such pictures as "The Solemn Land" singled him out as a remarkable artist.

Lawren Harris was born in Brantford, Ontario, in 1885. He studied art in Germany from 1908 to 1911 and for a very short time worked in New York as a magazine illustrator. He then came to Toronto and shocked shallow and fastidious viewers with his unsparing pictures of Toronto slums and the dreary row houses of coal miners in Cape Breton. As time went on his style changed and developed, becoming both more austere and more abstract. His interest in the free use of line and form is clearly shown in the picture, "Bylot Island" on the stamp.

The picture itself is another link with Canadian history. John Bylot, after whom the island was named, was a sailor and navigator who was with Henry Hudson in 1611 when the crew mutinied and set Hudson adrift in a small boat on Hudson Bay. Bylot may even have been one of the leaders in the mutiny. He had a grievance against Hudson who had recently reduced him from the rank of mate; and he became second-in-command of the mutineers. On the death of the leader, Bylot took charge and eventually got Hudson's ship home again. This won him a pardon for his share in the mutiny and he returned to Hudson Bay at least twice, commanding the *Discovery* in 1615 with William Baffin as his pilot.

A. Y. Jackson's "Alaska Highway between Watson Lake and Nelson," shown in a drab reproduction on the eight-cent stamp is typical of his paintings of the rugged Northland. He has sought subjects for his canvases in all parts of Canada even beyond the Arctic Circle. This particular picture shows his skill in selection of the essential features of a landscape and his facility in the capture of its rhythm. It shows a stretch of the strategic highway built between Dawson Creek, B.C., and Fairbanks, Alaska, during the Second World War. More than fifteen hundred miles of gravelled all-weather road was built in less than two years to enable military supplies to flow into Alaska which for a time was threatened with invasion by Japanese forces.

It was Harris who persuaded A. Y. Jackson (born in 1882) to come to Toronto from his native Montreal and who was the moving spirit behind the formation of the Group of Seven in 1920 when they held their first exhibition. The membership of the Group changed from time to time before it disbanded in 1933, but its members were the artists who first realized that Canada's vivid colours, vast distances, stark masses and clear atmosphere deserved the sweeping, ample and dynamic treatment that distinguished their work. A. Y. Jackson wrote, "We frankly abandoned attempts at literal painting . . . . We tried to emphasize colour, line and pattern. . . ."

What they did do was to give Canada its first vital school of nature painting, painting that was recognizably Canadian and which brought praise for the artists' work and attention to their country from all parts of the world where art is appreciated. MacDonald died in 1932, and after 1933 the members of the Group went their separate ways but they continued to paint, some of them for many years. Their work influenced younger painters, too, but art is always in the process of evolving. Styles change and interest moves towards newer, or at least different, patterns of expression. There is still much to attract the artist's eye in Canadian landscape and perhaps some later school of painters will return to it when the appeal of non-representational and purely abstract art has waned.

On September 18, 1970, there was issued a six-cent multicoloured stamp honouring the Group of Seven on the 50th anniversary of its foundation. It is a reproduction of the paint-

*The fifty-cent "Return from the Harvest Field" by Suzor-Côté, issued in
1969, and the six-cent Group of Seven stamp of 1970 (Arthur Lismer's
"Isles of Spruce").*

ing "Isles of Spruce" by Arthur Lismer, one of the original
members of the Group, who had also a long and influential
career as a teacher of art.

. . . . .

In 1971, on the centenary of her birth, Canada issued a
multicoloured stamp reproducing "The Big Raven," one of the
paintings of Emily Carr (1871-1945). Miss Carr was a
native of Victoria, B.C., who studied art in San Francisco,
London and Paris but who was always driven by her intense
love of her own country to return to a Canada that, for most
of her life, ignored her. For many years she was an eccentric
figure in Victoria — going to market pushing a dilapidated
baby carriage containing her pet monkey, Woo, and accompanied by six or eight exuberant English shepherd dogs which
she bred in order to eke out a small income.

Canada was not then very hospitable to the arts.
Young men of Emily Carr's generation who read books were
often considered wastrels — too lazy to do useful work. Her
own work was too "advanced" for most of her contemporaries,
who preferred the pretty and sentimental work of the decadent
late Victorian artists. But Emily Carr was a sturdy individual
who went her own way ignoring public opinion, ignoring the
critics, a blunt, downright individual who lived as she liked
and suffered fools not at all.

At one period she was much attracted by Indian life
and art. The Indians named her *Klee Wyck*, "Laughing
One," and their carvings and totems are the subject of a good
many of her best paintings, though she later went on to other
subjects. Towards the end of her life she won popular acclaim
for her writing, most of it autobiographical.

. . . . .

The six-cent stamp reproducing Emily Carr's "The Big Raven" and the seven-cent Paul Kane "Indian Encampment," both issued in 1971.

The latest stamp honouring a Canadian artist is the seven-cent multicoloured representation of Paul Kane's "An Indian Encampment amongst the Islands of Lake Huron" (1971). Kane was one of Canada's pioneer artists. He was born in County Cork, Ireland, in 1810 and brought to Canada as a small boy to grow up in York (Toronto). There he got a little education in the District Grammar School and learned to know the Indians and half-breeds who were a part of life in the muddy, dirty little village of about a hundred houses that made up the Toronto of that day.

He had a natural talent for drawing and was apprenticed to a manufacturer of furniture which it was his task to decorate. This occupation did not last long and he was soon earning money by painting bad portraits of such local worthies as the sheriff of Cobourg. Then followed a period of wandering in the United States where such odd jobs in art as he managed to find enabled him to scrape together funds to take him to Europe in 1841.

There he went from one art centre to another — Paris, Florence, Milan, Rome and London. He even managed a quick visit to the Middle East and North Africa. He copied European masterpieces, learned techniques and acquired skills. Nine years after leaving Canada he came home and at once set about the task of depicting Indian life and customs which was to occupy all his working life. He was encouraged by such patrons as Sir George Simpson, the governor of the Hudson's Bay Company, and by George William Allan who commissioned him to do one hundred paintings. It is this collection, now in the Royal Ontario Museum, that makes up the main body of Kane's work remaining in Canada. Other pictures have been lost or have gone to the United States.

Kane also wrote a long account of his journeys across the Canadian West. It was entitled *Wanderings of an Artist among the Indians of North America* and was originally published in 1859. It was later translated into French and Danish. A new illustrated edition has recently been issued in Canada.

Kane's work is valuable perhaps even more as a record of Indian life than as art. This is not to say that he was an inferior artist but rather to point out that he preserved for us a complete panorama of Indian life and customs that without his efforts would have been lost. His paintings and particularly his drawings are filled with accurately depicted detail by a highly skilled draughtsman. If his paintings have lost some of their appeal to the modern eye it may be because his years in Europe taught him a style that is no longer much liked or admired. His palette held only the colours popular in the Europe of his own day, the various shades of brown predominating. His Indian ponies recall the Arab or Greek horses he saw in the Mediterranean countries and his carefully posed Indian portrait subjects, except for costume and perhaps complexion, could represent dignified Italians, Frenchmen or Britons. In spite of these criticisms his work still holds our close attention and admiration, both for the painting itself and for the artist who accomplished it at the cost of much real hardship and discomfort. For, as he makes clear in his book, Kane spent a large part of his life among the Indians but he never really liked or admired them very much.

Failing eyesight brought his career to an end some years before he died in 1871. The stamp reproducing one of his best known pictures is a fitting memorial of one of our first artists, first not only in point of time but as a painter of international reputation.

Bibliography

Akins, T.B. *History of Halifax City.* Collections of the Nova Scotia Historical Society, Volume VIII. Halifax, 1895.

Bousfield, Hartwell. *Louis Riel: Rebel of the Western Frontier or Victim of Politics and Prejudice?* Toronto, 1969.

Brebner, John Bartlett. *The Explorers of North America, 1492-1806.* Cleveland, 1933.

_____. *Canada, A Modern History.* Ann Arbor, 1960.

Brown, George W. (gen. ed.). *Dictionary of Canadian Biography.* Toronto 1967, 1970.

Burpee, Lawrence J. (ed.). *An Historical Atlas of Canada.* Toronto, 1927.

Burt, A.L. *The Old Province of Quebec.* Toronto, 1933.

Calnek, W.A. and Savary, A.W. *History of the County of Annapolis.* Toronto, 1897.

Campbell, Marjorie Wilkins. *The Saskatchewan.* New York, 1950.

_____. *The North West Company.* Toronto, 1957.

Carr, Emily. *Klee Wyck.* Toronto, 1941.

Connell, Brian. *The Plains of Abraham.* London, 1959.

Costain, Thomas B. *The Great Intendant, Maclean's, Canada* (edited by Leslie Hannon). Toronto, 1960.

Creighton, Donald. *Dominion of the North.* Toronto, 1957.

_____. *Canada's First Century.* Toronto, 1970.

Daniells, Roy. *Alexander Mackenzie and the North West.* London, 1969.

Doughty, Arthur G. *The Acadian Exiles.* Toronto, 1920.

Fuller, Major General J.F.C. *A Military History of the Western World.* New York, 1955.

Griffiths, N.E.S. *The Acadian Deportation: Deliberate Perfidy or Cruel Necessity.* Toronto, 1969.

Heinleroff-Schleicher, Edythe. *M.C.: A Portrayal of Emily Carr.* Toronto, 1969.

Hibbert, Christopher. *Wolfe at Quebec.* London, 1959.

Hill, Douglas. *The Opening of the Canadian West.* London, 1967.

Hutchinson, Bruce. *The Fraser.* Toronto, 1950.

Kane, Paul. *Wanderings of an Artist among the Indians of North America.* Toronto, 1925.

Kavanagh, Martin. *La Vérendrye: His Life and Times.* Brandon, 1967.

Knight, James (ed.). *The Formative Years.* Toronto, 1967.

Lower, Arthur R.M. *Canadians in the Making.* Toronto, 1958.

Mackay, Douglas. *The Honourable Company.* Toronto, 1936.

Macksey, Kenneth. *The Shadow of Vimy Ridge.* Toronto, 1965.

MacMechan, Archibald McK. *The Winning of Popular Government.* Toronto, 1920.

McKee, Alexander. *Vimy Ridge.* London, 1966.

Metcalf, Vicky. *Journey Fantastic.* Toronto, 1969.
Morton, W.L. *The Critical Years.* Toronto, 1964.
Murdock, Beamish. *History of Nova Scotia.* n.p. 1865.
Osler, E.B. *The Man Who Had to Hang Louis Riel.* Toronto, 1961.
Pethick, Derek. *Victoria, the Fort.* Vancouver, 1968.
Radall, Thomas H. *The Path of Destiny.* Toronto, 1957.
Reid, J.H. Stewart, McNaught, Kenneth and Crowe, Harry S. *A Source Book of Canadian History.* Toronto, 1964.
Ryerson, Egerton. *The Loyalists of America and Their Times.* Toronto, 1880.
Robson, Albert H. *Canadian Landscape Painters.* Toronto, 1932.
Saunders, Edward Manning. *Three Premiers of Nova Scotia.* Toronto, 1909.
Swettenham, John. *To Seize the Victory.* Toronto, 1965.
Vail, Philip. *The Magnificent Adventure of Alexander Mackenzie.* New York, 1964.
Way, Ronald L. *The Day of Crysler's Farm.* Morrisburg, n.d.
Williams. Norman Lloyd. *Sir Walter Raleigh.* London, 1962.
Wilson, Richard. (ed.). *Stories from Hakluyt.* London, 1921.
Woodcock, George. *Canada & the Canadians.* London, 1970.
Wright, Esther Clark. *The Saint John River.* Toronto, 1949.

Index